Bob Jones U

ERRORS

on

Bible Preservation

A Critique of

Bible Preservation &
the Providence of God

Pastor D. A. Waite, Th.D., Ph.D.

Published by

THE BIBLE FOR TODAY PRESS
900 Park Avenue
Collingswood, New Jersey 08108
U.S.A.

Church Phone: 856-854-4747
BFT Phone: 856-854-4452
Orders: 1-800-John 10:9
E-mail: BFT@BibleForToday.org
Website: www.BibleForToday.org
Fax: 856-854-2464

**We Use and Defend
the King James Bible**

**February, 2006
BFT #3259**

Copyright, 2006
All Rights Reserved

ISBN #1-56848-053-9

Acknowledgments

I wish to thank and to acknowledge the assistance of the following people:

- **Dianne W. Cosby**, for typing these radio messages from the original cassette tapes and putting them in computer format. They were all originally heard around the world via shortwave radio;

- **Yvonne Sanborn Waite**, my wife, who encouraged the publication of these radio messages, read the manuscript, and gave helpful suggestions;

- **Barbara Egan**, our BIBLE FOR TODAY secretary who proofread the manuscript and straightened out some spellings and many other things that should be corrected;

- **Loretta Smith**, a former attender of our Bible For Today Baptist Church, who moved out of state, but was still able and willing to help in this task. She read the manuscript and suggested improvements;

- **Daniel S. Waite**, one of our sons, and the Assistant to the BIBLE FOR TODAY Director, who kept my computer in working order, helped guide the book through the printing process, and in other ways.

- **Pastor Alan Panek**, one of our BIBLE FOR TODAY employees who read the manuscript and gave some needed corrections.

Foreword

- The material in this present book was first delivered by way of a series of thirty-minute radio broadcasts which went out by AM and FM radio, by Internet, and by shortwave around the world. For this reason, I have repeated some things more frequently than usual so that the **STATEMENT** that I am answering will be supplied with the necessary information, even though it has been given in earlier **COMMENTS**.

- The book that I am critiquing, *Bible Preservation and the Providence of God* (BPPG), is very important because it is the first time that the battle against Bible preservation has moved clearly to Bob Jones University (BJU), since the book's two writers have been employed by BJU. One of the authors, Samuel Schnaiter, is the Chairman of the Ancient Languages Department of BJU. I have done this on two previous occasions by means of radio broadcasts. I have refuted his BJU Ph.D. dissertation, available on four, two-hour audio cassettes **(BFT #139-142 @ $12.00+$4 S&H)**. I have refuted his sermon on Bible texts and translations as delivered at Heritage Bible Church in Greer, SC in the a.m. and p.m. services on August 23, 1998, available on six, two-hour audio cassettes **(BFT #146-151 @ $18.00+$4 S&H)**.

- Though two former books had the endorsement of Bob Jones III, then President of Bob Jones University (BJU), and were authored by many BJU graduates, trustee board members, cooperating board members, teachers, and friends, they were not written exclusively by men who were in the employ of BJU. That first book was called *From the Mind of God to the Mind of Man*. The second book was called *God's Word in Our Hands—The Bible Preserved For Us*. Though "*Preserved*" is in the title of this second book, it is against true "<u>Bible Preservation</u>."

- The first book was answered in my book, *Fundamentalist Mis-Information on Bible Versions* **(BFT #2974 @ $7+$4**

S&H). The second book was answered in my book, *Fundamentalist Deception on Bible Preservation* (BFT #3234 @ $8+$4 S&H). The term *"Deception"* was used in the title because, in reality, *God's Word in Our Hands* is against true "**Bible Preservation**" though it claims to be in favor of it.

• Sadly, the present book under review follows the same deception as *God's Word in Our Hands*, namely, it is against true "**Bible Preservation**." This has been the official position of Bob Jones University against true "**Bible Preservation**" for a number of years. It was first enunciated in the BJU doctoral dissertation of one of the present writers, Samuel Schnaiter, in the 1980's. This false position was approved by his doctoral dissertation committee. This false position of BJU has had a pervasive influence on Bible institutes, colleges, universities, churches, and individuals both in the United States and on many of the mission fields of the world. This influence must be combated and corrected by the presentation of the truth about true "**Bible Preservation**." This present review seeks to do just that. It is hoped that good schools that hold to the King James Bible and to the preservation of the original Hebrew, Aramaic, and Greek **Words** underlying it–such as Heritage Baptist University, Maryland Baptist Bible College, Fairhaven Baptist Bible College, Emmanuel Baptist Theological Seminary, and others--will continue to stand fast for these Biblical truths.

• Unless otherwise noted, any emphasis by means of the use of **bold**, underlining, or **both** has been added to the quotations.

Sincerely yours for God's **Words**,

D. a. Waite

Pastor D. A. Waite, Th.D., Ph.D.
Bible For Today Baptist Church, and
Director, The BIBLE FOR TODAY, Incorporated

Table of Contents

Bob Jones University's

ERRORS

on Bible Preservation

Introductory Remarks

In my opinion, this book contains at least two hundred twelve false or misleading statements on Bible Preservation or related topics concerning the Bible. Before looking into these statements, I would like to say a few things by way of introduction to the book.

The Book's Connection with Bob Jones University. Two staff members of Bob Jones University have written a book called *Bible Preservation and the Providence of God*. Because of the authors' affiliation with Bob Jones University (BJU), that school must agree enough with the book to have permitted these men to have written it. There is no disclaimer in the book to the effect that though the writers are connected with BJU, the book sets forth only the opinions of the authors and these views are not necessarily those of the school with which they are affiliated. Because of the absence of such a disclaimer, I am assuming that these views represent those of BJU as well. My analysis will therefore be called *"Bob Jones University's Errors on Bible Preservation."*

The Writers. The names of the two writers are Samuel Schnaiter and Ron Tagliapietra. When the book was published, both of these men were connected with Bob Jones University (BJU).

Samuel Schnaiter has been at Bob Jones University for many years. He received his Ph.D. from there in 1980. His doctoral dissertation was about New Testament Textual Criticism. I have a copy of this dissertation and have read it thoroughly. I have strong disagreements with it in many areas. Since 1970 he has been on the faculty of Bob Jones University. At the time of writing, he was both a Professor of New Testament Language and Literature and the Chairman of the University's Ancient Languages Department.

Ron Tagliapietra has gone to the following schools: (1) Central College, (2) University of Oregon, (3) Pillsbury Baptist Bible College and (4) Bob Jones University. As of the publication date of this book, he had been writing books for the Bob Jones University Press for twelve years. Both of these men are on the staff of Bob Jones University.

The Source of the Book. I got this book from Bob Jones University. They sell it in their bookstore. There is no disclaimer on the book, as on other books sold in the school's bookstore, that states that the school does not necessarily approve of all that is written in this book. Many books sold in the school's bookstore have a disclaimer on them. They say that Bob Jones University does not necessarily agree with everything within the particular book. Because there is no such disclaimer, it means that Bob Jones University does not disagree with the views expressed in this book. In other words, this book has Bob Jones University's blessings.

The Cost of the Book. The book has approximately three hundred fifty pages. In my opinion it is way overpriced. It is a **paperback** book that costs $22.99 plus $6.50 for shipping and handling. That is a total of **$29.49** for the book. By way of contrast, my own book, *Defending the King James Bible*, is a **hardback** book of about the same number of pages (three hundred fifty) and we sell it for $12.00 plus $5.00 shipping and handling for a total of only **$17.00**.

The Outline of the Book. The twelve chapters are divided into three units followed by several appendices. The pages referred to in this outline are pages in the book under review and are not the pages in this critique.

Introduction 7

Unit I

Preservation of Scripture 13

Unit II

Transmission of Scripture 71

Unit III

Translation of Scripture 185

Two Hundred Twelve Misleading Statements

Introduction

Though there may be many more false or misleading statements in this book, I have limited myself to the following two hundred twelve.

Not Fair and Balanced

STATEMENT #1: (p. 1). They say that they want to have a "*fair handling*" of the subject. They say there is an inordinate amount of criticism and they want to have a "*fair handling*."

COMMENT #1: I do not think it is a "*fair handling*" of the Bible, including Bible Preservation. They do not believe the <u>Words</u> of Hebrew, Aramaic, and Greek have been preserved to this day. They believe only the "*ideas, thoughts, concepts, message, truth, or teachings*"of the original languages have been preserved.

STATEMENT #2: (p. 9). "*In 1881 when Westcott and Hort produced what they considered to be a carefully edited Greek text, the conflict revived in opposition to their text. As far as we know, no Fundamentalist has written a book that articulates a good biblical <u>balance</u> in this complicated issue.*"

COMMENT #2:

> It is not possible to <u>*balance*</u> two things that are completely opposite. Either the <u>Words</u> of the Traditional Received Greek Text and the Traditional Masoretic Hebrew Text underlying the King James Bible are the right <u>Words</u> or they are the wrong <u>Words</u>. Either the words of the Critical Greek Texts are the right words or they are the wrong words. You cannot balance truth with error. Either one is true and the other is false, or one is false and the other is true. You cannot have a balance in this situation. It is not possible.

Little Clarity More Defense

STATEMENT #3: (p. 9). "*The following, then, is intended to be something of a <u>reference manual</u> to <u>clarify</u> and evaluate the opposing* *arguments of this conflict from a Fundamentalist perspective.*"

COMMENT #3: If they can "*clarify*," that is one thing. Have they really "*clarified*" this problem? I do not think so. As far as this book being a "*reference manual*," I do not believe it is a good "*manual*." I believe it is a flawed "*manual*."

STATEMENT #4: (p. 9). "*We are not irretrievably committed to defending or advancing one position over another in this conflict.*"

COMMENT #4: Whom are they trying to impress? I do not believe that for a moment. I believe they are "*irretrievably committed to defending or advancing*" the Critical Text either of Westcott and Hort, United Bible Societies, or Nestle/Aland. This has been done by Samuel Schnaiter and other faculty members at Bob Jones University ever since the arrival on the faculty of Dr. Charles Brokenshire who was either Dean or Professor from 1943 to 1954.

STATEMENT #5: (p. 9). "*In fact the co-authors do not favor the same theory.*"

COMMENT #5: That is an interesting statement, but the result of this book is their development of a single theory, and that an erroneous one, as will be seen throughout this analysis. This statement attempts to disarm the reader into thinking that Bob Jones University somehow has forsaken its dogmatic position in favor of the Greek Critical Text when, in fact, they have not done so, nor will they do so in the future I predict. This false **theory** has too great a foothold on that school and on its graduates that are scattered in other schools, pastorates, and the mission fields of the world.

STATEMENT #6: (p. 9). "*We hope that our attempt will shed light on the issue, provide balance, and prove that we prefer to sort out what is crucial to hold as part of the Bible believer's creed as distinguished from mere interpretive opinion.*"

COMMENT #6: As I said before, I do not believe you can "*balance*" truth with error. This is what we have here when dealing with the **Words** of the Bible. I believe the Hebrew, Aramaic, and Greek **Words** that underlie our King James Bible are true and proper **Words**. I believe the Hebrew, Aramaic, and Greek **Words** underlying the modern versions that differ from those underlying the King James Bible are false and improper words. In the New Testament, Dr. Jack Moorman has outlined over 8,000 differences between the Greek Text of Nestle/Aland and the Greek Text underlying the King James Bible. This book of over 500-large-pages on "*8,000 Differences*" is available from the BIBLE FOR TODAY for a gift of **$65.00 + $7.50 S&H.** It is **BFT #3084.**

Much "Interpretive Opinion" Here

STATEMENT #7: (p. 9) "*. . . as distinguished from mere interpretive opinion.*"

COMMENT #7: I do not give "*interpretive opinion.*" I give factual evidence.

Where Is Their "Written Word"?

STATEMENT #8: (p. 10). "*That which distinguishes Bible believing Christians from the world of men is their commitment to the written Word of God as their sole authority. Properly understood, the Bible is the final appeal in all matters on which it speaks to and commands men, . . .*"

COMMENT #8: They are committed to the "*written Word of God,*" but where is the "*written Word of God*" for them? Is it the Hebrew, Aramaic, and Greek **Words** which underlie our King James Bible which I believe are the truth? Or is it the Hebrew and Greek **Words** that underlie the false versions which is their opinion? What are the "*written Words*"? The writers say they are committed to "*the written Word of God*" but never define it. With their false view of Bible preservation, they have removed "*written Words*" for the false basis of written "*ideas, thoughts, concepts, message, truth, or teachings.*" This is serious error.

STATEMENT #9: (p. 10). "*. . . much is passed off as God's authority which amounts to no more than men's impulses or opinions or interpretations of God's authority.*"

COMMENT #9: I do not want simply "*men's impulses or opinions or interpretations of God's authority.*" I want the Hebrew, Aramaic and Greek **Words** which underlie the King James Bible. These are the **Words** God has preserved for us, not merely the "*ideas, thoughts, concepts, message, truth, or teachings.*"

STATEMENT #10: (p. 10). "*Fifteen years ago, when we became independently interested in this subject, . .*"

COMMENT #10: This book came out in 2002. "*Fifteen years ago*" would be 1987. That is when the authors began to think about writing a book on this subject.

STATEMENT #11: (p. 11). "*What remains are a few dozen troubling questions that come up in the minds of thoughtful, godly people when they are made aware of this subject and its controversies.*"

COMMENT #11: There are many more than "*a few dozen troubling questions*" in these "*controversies.*"

Statement #12: (p. 11). *"At one time such debate was considered appropriate only for seminary students."*

COMMENT #12: That is what they used to say. Now it is a subject on which every born-again Christian should be informed.

Theirs Is An "Extreme Position"

STATEMENT #13: (p. 11). *"However, because the extreme positions have been advanced boldly and publicly, most Christians still struggle with textual issues at least occasionally."*

COMMENT #13: There are at least two "extreme positions" on the Bible texts, translations, and preservation.

(1) Extreme Position #1. The Peter Ruckman position is one of the **extreme positions** on this subject. He is a graduate of Bob Jones University. He pastors a church in Pensacola, Florida. He believes that the King James Bible corrects the original Hebrew and Greek from which it was taken and contains *"advanced revelation."* The authors also believe my position is extreme, but it is not. They consider my book, *Defending the King James Bible*, as being an extreme position. It is contrary to Ruckmanism. It is not extreme at all. It is based upon facts and documents.

(2) Extreme Position #2. Another "**extreme position**" is the position of Bob Jones University and the writers of this book. They reject the **Words** on which the King James Bible is based and claim God has not promised to preserve His Hebrew, Aramaic, and Greek **Words**, nor has He done so. He has only preserved the *"ideas, thoughts, concepts, message, truth, or teachings"* of His **Words**, but not the exact **Words** themselves.

"All Sides" Not Presented

STATEMENT #14: (p. 11). *"This means that anyone wanting to hear all sides of the debate has to read at least a half dozen books."*

COMMENT #14: I do not think you need to "*hear all sides of the debate*." A person should get my own book, *Defending the King James Bible* which mentions all of the various sides and comes down on the correct side. I hope you will get a copy of it. It is **BFT #1594**. At this writing, it is in its 9th printing, hardback edition. It is 350 pages for a gift of **$12.00 plus $5.00 S&H.** That will give you the position that I take. I believe in the preservation of the **Words** of Scripture and not just the *"ideas, thoughts, concepts, message, truth, or teachings."* It talks about the other position of Westcott and Hort that I was taught at Dallas Theological Seminary. You do not need a half dozen books to see the picture. That one book will do it.

STATEMENT #15: (p. 11). *"We hope (if only by putting the brakes on each other's interests) to provide a useful textbook in a calm encyclopedic style that will **help people understand the issues** and evaluate the positions."*

COMMENT #15: I do not believe they achieved this purpose in their book of helping people "**understand the issues**" involved in the area of Bible preservation. They did not even present the true position of the preservation of the original Hebrew, Aramaic, and Greek **Words** of the Bible.

STATEMENT #16: (p. 11). *"What follows is an attempt to: (1) Distinguish between the teachings of the **Word** of God on this subject and the opinions (however strongly held) of men. (2) Build up believers as they see how God has providentially directed the discovery of manuscript evidence to vindicate His own promise of preservation. (3) Present the major viewpoints; clarifying their strengths, weaknesses and the issues involved. (4) Answer the troublesome questions about textual and transnational matters of the New Testament."*

COMMENT #16: I shall make comments and take issue with each of these four attempts as they occur in the book.

Statements on Unit I Preservation of Scripture

Their "Preservation" Is False

This section is where "*the rubber meets the road*" as they say. This book's position on Bible preservation is erroneous and deceptive. Both the words "*Preservation*" and "*Scripture*" are deceptively designed. What they talk about is not "*preservation.*" What they talk about in this unit is not "*Scripture,*" which really includes the original Hebrew, Aramaic and Greek <u>Words</u> of "*Scripture.*" These writers do not believe that those <u>Words</u> have been preserved for today.

There Are No "Text Types"

STATEMENT #17: (p. 13). "*We know dozens of pastors who are in a <u>quandary</u> about <u>text types</u> and translations.*"

COMMENT #17: If these pastors would read my book, *Defending the King James Bible*, they would no longer be in a "<u>*quandary.*</u>" If they read their book, they would still be in a "<u>*quandary.*</u>" I do not believe there are any "<u>*text types*</u>" of Greek manuscripts, only individual manuscripts.

They Deny Preserved "Words"

STATEMENT #18: p. 14). "*. . . issues discussed in Units 2 and 3 also because they provide evidence that God has indeed <u>preserved His Word</u> as He promised.*"

COMMENT #18:

That is the first red flag. When you see in their book the words "<u>*preserved His word,*</u>" do not dare believe they mean God has preserved His original Hebrew, Aramaic, and Greek <u>Words</u>. They have taken a fly-by-night definition of "Word." They believe it means only the "*ideas, thoughts, concepts, message, truth, or teachings,*" but not the original <u>Words</u>. They have extrapolated. They have added to the meaning of the word, Word. In the Bible, whenever God talks about the <u>Word</u> of God he means the <u>Words</u> of God. These two terms are co-equal. They are co-extensive. They are exactly the same.

For years, and decades, since I have been saved in 1944 by God's grace, when we referred to the Word of God we meant the Words of God. There was never any difference between those two phrases. Not so with these men from Bob Jones University, Detroit Baptist Seminary, Central Baptist Seminary, Calvary Baptist Seminary and the other Fundamental schools that follow their views. These colleges and universities are Fundamentalist in other areas but not in the area of what is known in theology as Bibliology.

They take a similar view of the modernists and apostates as far as Bible preservation is concerned. Both these Fundamentalists and the apostates deny that the original Hebrew, Aramaic, and Greek Words have been preserved to this day. God has promised that He would preserve His Words and He has kept that promise in the Words underlying the King James Bible.

What do you think they mean by the term "*His Word*"? They do not mean his Words. In the original Bible, God spoke in the Words of Hebrew, Aramaic, and Greek. God has promised to preserve those Words. These writers say God promised only to preserve His Word, by which they mean only His "*ideas, thoughts, concepts, message, truth, or teachings*" but not His original Words. This is gross and serious error, heresy, and apostasy!

Watch out for these men who are deceptive in their use of terms. Any debater before he debates another team always defines his terms so that both sides agree on those definitions and are debating the same thing. Such clear definitions are absent in the present book as well as the other two Bob Jones University sanctioned books, *From the Mind of God to the Mind of Man* and *God's Word in our Hands--the Bible Preserved for Us*. Both these last two books were edited by men closely connected with BJU, Dr. J. B. Williams and Randolph Shaylor.

The writers should define such important terms at the very beginning so the reader would not have to read any further than the introduction of this book and see where these men are coming from. They should have done the same for these other two BJU-sanctioned books mentioned above.

CHAPTER 1

DOCTRINE OF THE BIBLE

Denial of True "Words Preservation"

STATEMENT #19: (p. 15). [This is from Chapter One "The Doctrine of the Bible"] "*This Chapter presents the doctrines of inspiration and preservation from Scripture.*"

COMMENT #19: Though their view of **inspiration** might be correct, they have adopted an heretical and apostate view of Bible preservation.

STATEMENT #20: (p. 16). *"Jesus said 'Thy __Word__ is truth' (John 17:17) which makes it __infallible__. It is __inerrant__ or free from error because God cannot lie."*

COMMENT #20: I agree with that statement if "__Word__" is properly defined as "__Words.__" I would disagree if the authors put their false definition on it as merely the *"ideas, thoughts, concepts, message, truth, or teachings,"* but not the original Hebrew, Aramaic, and Greek __Words__. Furthermore, since they find errors in the __Words__ of Hebrew, Aramaic, and Greek that we have today, how can they be certain that the original __Words__ were either "__infallible__" or "__inerrant__" except by faith?

STATEMENT #21: (p. 16). [They are referring to John 10:35b] *"A document with errors can certainly be '__broken__' . . ."*

COMMENT #21: I would agree with that. If the *"Scripture cannot be __broken__,"* this is a reference to perfect plenary, verbal preservation of the original __Words__. It cannot refer, as they make it refer, only to God's *"ideas, thoughts, concepts, message, truth, or teachings."* I do not believe the writers are applying accurately John 10:35b to this subject.

"Teaching" Inerrant, but Not Words

STATEMENT #22: (p. 16) *"The __teaching__ of Scripture is inerrant and infallible, . . ."*

COMMENT #22: Notice they use the word "__teaching.__" This is just one more undefined term wherein they deny the preservation of the __Words__ of the originals. It can be placed right along with their other meanings for the "__word__" of God like *"ideas, thoughts, concepts, message, truth, or teachings,"* but not the original __Words__. They do not believe that God has preserved His Hebrew, Aramaic, and Greek __Words__ to this day, but only the *"ideas, thoughts, concepts, message, truth, or teachings"* are inerrant and infallible.

STATEMENT #23: (p. 16). [Speaking of the Lord Jesus Christ] *"He claimed that the __words__ and even the portions of words (jots and tittles) are __reliable__, not just the __teaching__."*

COMMENT #23: Notice that they use "__words__" and even "__portions of words__," but they do not declare them to be "__inerrant Words__," but just "__reliable.__" There is a world of difference between "__reliable__" and "__inerrant.__" They are very clever and deceptive in the use of this kind of language in order to confuse the undiscerning who read their book.

STATEMENT #24: (p. 17) *"The Scripture is completely, infallibly, and verbally inspired. . . . It is nevertheless inerrant in regard to every deception* *of doctrine, history, and science that it __affirms__."*

COMMENT #24: I would agree with the first sentence. Their limitation of inerrancy is weak using the word "__*affirms*__." I attended, as a credentialed reporter, the International Congress on Evangelism that Billy Graham had in Switzerland many years ago. They used the phrase that the Bible was accurate "*in all the things it affirmed.*" What does it "__affirm__"? What does it say? What does it teach? That's a weak position and a weak word. It is accurate in all it **says** not just all it __affirms__. That is very weak terminology.

Not Given "Word By Word"?

STATEMENT #25: (page 18) *"The second conclusion to be drawn is that God did not dictate the New Testament __word by word__."*

COMMENT #25:

I differ with that. I believe that God did dictate word-by-word. He may have used the author's vocabulary so that Peter sounded like Peter, and John sounded like John and Paul sounded like Paul. He gave them the __Words__. He did not tell them to use their own words. No, He gave every single word and that's why it is God's __Words__ that have been promised to be preserved and have been preserved. Those __Words__ of Hebrew, Aramaic, and Greek that underlie our King James Bible are the preserved original __Words__.

"Message" Is Not Enough

STATEMENT #26: (page 19) [speaking of the writers of Scripture] *"The result is what they spoke (and later wrote) is the __message__ of God to man."*

COMMENT #26: This is absolutely false. The authors of the Old and New Testaments did not simply write the "__message__" of God to men. They wrote the __Words__ of God to men. That's the trouble of that phony title of that first book by mostly Bob Jones University teachers or graduates entitled *From the __Mind__ of God to the Mind of Man.* It is not God's __*mind*__. It is from the __Words__ of God to the words of man. This idea of God's speaking and later writing only the "__*message*__" of God is false and deceptive. It must be the exact Hebrew, Aramaic, and Greek __Words__ He gave to us. These preserved Hebrew, Aramaic, and Greek __Words__ have been translated accurately for us into the English language in our King James Bible.

STATEMENT #27: (page 19) *"... this word [graphe] has reference to the inspired __word__ of God either in part or the whole. .... The __lesson__ here is the inspired Scripture is __authoritative__."*

COMMENT #27: Here again it is not the "God-breathed" "message, idea, thought, or teaching." It is the "God-breathed" __WORDS__.

PASA GRAPHE THEOPNEUSTOS. They are the three Greek words that are used in 2 Timothy 3:16. That which has been written down are the **Words** not just the "*ideas, thoughts, concepts, message, truth, or teachings.*" The "*lesson*" is not merely that the Bible is "*authoritative.*" It is far more than that. It is Word-for-Word what God Himself breathed out.

Leaving "God" Out of "Inspiration"

STATEMENT #28: (page 19) "*In 2 Timothy 3:16, we are told of the origin of the graphe. It is the product of the divine breath of God as evidenced by the word THEOPNEUSTOS which translates 'given by inspiration.'*"

COMMENT #28:

The word, THEOPNEUSTOS is not translated "*given by inspiration*" in 2 Timothy 3:16. It is translated "*given by inspiration of God.*" The word is made up of THEOS, which is God, and PNEUSTOS, which is the participle of PNEO which means to breathe. You cannot leave out God in the breathing-out of His **Words**.

STATEMENT #29: (p. 20) "*The Bible, then, is authoritative as the inspired Word of God.*"

COMMENT #29: Notice once again the use of "**Word**" of God. They do not mean the "**Words**" of God. To me, and in the Bible, both terms refer to the "**Words**" of God, but not to these writers or to Bob Jones University that they represent. When they use "**Word**," they redefine it, but they do not tell you they are redefining it. In effect they are subverting the "**Word**." They are secretly, deceitfully, and surreptitiously modifying "**Word**" into the false meaning of only the "*ideas, thoughts, concepts, message, truth, or teachings,*" but not "**Words.**" The Bible is more than merely "**authoritative.**" This is a weak word used to diminish the promise of the preservation of the original Hebrew, Aramaic, and Greek **Words** of the Bible. What remains of those original Words can be termed by them as only "**authoritative**" but not accurately preserved as **Words**.

"Preserved . . . Word" not Words

STATEMENT #30: (p. 20) [talking about preservation] "*With the completion of the revelation, God preserved his Word first by having his people recognize the inspired writings as divine, and then by protecting them from destruction and even from corruption.*"

COMMENT #30: Here again they are stating only that "**God preserved His Word**" instead of preserving His "**Words.**" By this term, **Word**, they believe that God has **preserved** only His "*ideas, thoughts, concepts,* *message, truth, or teachings."* This is the false view of these two men employed by Bob Jones University and of the school itself. They deny that God has preserved His original Hebrew, Aramaic, and Greek "<u>Words</u>." It is as simple as that. Should I not be irate at this? Should I not be anxious about this? Should I not be stirred up about this? As a preacher of the Gospel and pastor of the **Bible For Today Baptist Church** here in Collingswood, New Jersey, I am irate, stirred up, and angry at their deceptive redefinition of the meaning of "<u>Word</u>." This is what the heretical neo-orthodox theologians did. They used the same terms as the Fundamentalists use, but they changed the meaning of each of the terms in order to confuse their audiences into believing they were orthodox in their beliefs. They redefined such terms as *"resurrection, divinity of Christ, salvation"* and other theological terms. The people who were listening to these terms thought that they were using them with the orthodox meaning. They were not aware that they had redefined those terms to mean completely different things.

Casual readers of this present book, *Bible Preservation and the Providence of God*, might think these writers, and Bob Jones University, whom they represent, really believe in *"Bible preservation."* They redefine *"Bible"* as being only the *"ideas, thoughts, concepts, message, truth, or teachings"* found in the Bible, but not the Hebrew, Aramaic, and Greek "<u>Words</u>" originally given in the Bible. That is not the *"Bible"* and it is not *"Preservation."*

"Preserved" His Word, not <u>Words</u>

STATEMENT #31: (p. 23) *"The Lord has clearly <u>preserved His</u> <u>Word</u> through the canon of Scripture."*

      COMMENT #31: Here again they say "<u>preserved His</u> <u>Word</u>." They mean by this only the *"ideas, thoughts, concepts, message, truth, or teachings"* of the Bible, but not its original "<u>Words</u>."

      STATEMENT #32: (p. 23) [talking about eternal preservation] *"The Scripture also has much to say concerning <u>its own preservation</u>. The Bible makes clear that God's <u>Word</u> will survive the most bitter and determined opposition to it imaginable."*

      COMMENT #32: Here again "<u>Word</u>" is used, by which is meant only the *"ideas, thoughts, concepts, message, truth, or teachings"* of the Bible, but not its original "<u>Words</u>." This is their mistaken view of the Bible's "<u>own preservation</u>."

      STATEMENT #33: (p. 23) *"Jesus Himself indicated that the <u>Scripture</u> will always be available for man to live by (Matthew 4:4)."*

      COMMENT #33: Notice that the word "<u>Scripture</u>" is used instead of the original "<u>Words</u>" found therein. By their redefinition, they mean merely the *"ideas, thoughts, concepts, message, truth, or teachings"* of the Bible, but not its original "Words."

STATEMENT #34: (p. 23) *"The doctrine that God's Word remains forever is the doctrine that it is eternal."*

COMMENT #34: Here again "Word" is used, by which is meant only the *"ideas, thoughts, concepts, message, truth, or teachings"* of the Bible, but not its original "Words." For them, only God's "*Word*" is "eternal," but not the original Hebrew, Aramaic, and Greek Words.

STATEMENT #35: (p. 23) *"We know that 'in the beginning was the Word' (John 1:1), and in fact, 'Thy word is true from the beginning' (Psalm 119). This means that the Word has existed from eternity past in heaven."*

COMMENT #35: Here again "Word" is used, by which is meant only the *"ideas, thoughts, concepts, message, truth, or teachings"* of the Bible, but not its original Hebrew, Aramaic, and Greek "Words."

Only "Substantially" the "Word"?

STATEMENT #36: (p. 24) *". . . those who want God's Word are not now, nor ever will be, substantially without the Word of God."*

COMMENT #36: They say that we will never be "*substantially*" without the "Word" of God. Notice the qualification, "substantially without the Word of God." They do not say the "Words of God." Here again "Word" is used, by which is meant only the *"ideas, thoughts, concepts, message, truth, or teachings"* of the Bible, but not its original "Words." Schnaiter and Tagliapietra do not believe that God has promised to preserve His Greek, Aramaic, and Hebrew Words. That's the first error that they make. God **did** promise to preserve his Hebrew, Aramaic, and Greek Words that He gave to us in the very beginning of the Bible. That is the first error.

> Secondly, they do not believe he HAS preserved His original Greek, Aramaic, and Hebrew Words. Not only do they not believe God PROMISED to preserve His Words, but also they believe God DID NOT preserve His Words, but only his *"ideas, thoughts, concepts, message, truth, or teachings."* In this way, they believe they have only "*substantially*" (but not perfectly and totally) the "Word" of God. What a defective position of Bible preservation!

By their use of the word "*substantially*," they mean we do not have everything. We definitely do not have the original "Words" according to them. In their book, Schnaiter and Tagliapietra show that they believe that there are scribal errors in the Bible. They call them "typos." They may have scribal errors or "typos" in the manuscripts that they use. I would agree that there are many scribal errors in the manuscripts that the Westcott and Hort Text used.

The Hebrew, Aramaic, and Greek <u>**Words**</u> that underlie our King James Bible are not only "*<u>substantially</u>*" correct, but they are perfectly correct. I believe those "<u>**Words**</u>" have been preserved down to the letter. God has preserved every single <u>word</u> of Hebrew, Aramaic, and Greek that underlies our King James Bible. That is what I believe the Bible teaches. That is what I believe the results have shown. I believe that the <u>**Words**</u> of Hebrew, Aramaic, and Greek which underlie our King James Bible are the preserved, inerrant, infallible, inspired original "<u>**Words**</u>" of the Bible. I also believe that the King James Bible is the only correct and accurate translation of those original Hebrew, Aramaic, and Greek "<u>**Words**</u>" in the English language. Therefore I can hold up my King James Bible and say it is God's "<u>**Words**</u>" in English. We can hold it up and thank God, because of its accurate translation, we have His "<u>**Words**</u>" properly translated and thus preserved for us in English in our King James Bible.

STATEMENT #37: (p. 24) [referring to Deuteronomy 8:3] "*. . . then that <u>Word</u> would have to be available for men in every age.*"

COMMENT #37: Though "<u>word</u>" is used in Deuteronomy 8:3, it means the same as the "<u>**Words**</u>" of God. When these writers use "<u>**Word**</u>," however, they mean only the "*ideas, thoughts, concepts, message, truth, or teachings*" of the Bible, but not its original Hebrew, Aramaic, and Greek "<u>**Words**</u>." The "<u>**Words**</u>" must be and should be available in every age, and it was available. Not that everyone had the "<u>**Words**</u>" of God, but the Hebrew <u>**Words**</u>, the Aramaic <u>**Words**</u>, and the Greek <u>**Words**</u> were available. Not that everyone had a copy, but they were available if they searched them out.

STATEMENT #38: (p. 24) "*This means that God's <u>Word</u> was preserved for the Jews first in Hebrew and then in the <u>Greek Old Testaments</u> . . . .*"

COMMENT #38: Here again "<u>Word</u>" is used, by which is meant only the "*ideas, thoughts, concepts, message, truth, or teachings*" of the Bible, but not its original "<u>**Words**</u>."

> The preservation of Scripture has nothing to do with the flawed and defective <u>Greek Old Testament</u>. He believes it was made B.C. I believe that the <u>Greek Old Testament</u> was a product of Origen in Alexandria, Egypt in the early 200's A.D.

More Than "Minor Differences"

STATEMENT #39: (p. 24) "*But we will also find that God has been true to his promises--to preserve His <u>Word</u> for His people--in spite of those* *minor differences*."

COMMENT #39: Here again "<u>Word</u>" is used, by which is meant only the "*ideas, thoughts, concepts, message, truth, or teachings*" of the Bible, but not its original "<u>Words</u>." If there are "*<u>differences</u>*," then he does not believe God has preserved His "<u>Words</u>" because of the "*<u>minor differences</u>*." We must distinguish between what "<u>Words</u>" God has preserved and what words are not His. That is why we should argue and debate the Greek text of the New Testament. It is not the text of Westcott and Hort. It is not the text of the United Bible Societies. It is not the text of Nestle/Aland. The true original "<u>Words</u>" of the New Testament are the "<u>Words</u>" which underlie our King James Bible.

STATEMENT #40: (p. 25) "*God's promises to <u>preserve his word</u> are no less applicable to those situations than to that of people of <u>varying languages</u>.*"

COMMENT #40: Here again these writers use the expression "**<u>preserve His Word</u>**" to mean only the "*ideas, thoughts, concepts, message, truth, or teachings*" of the Bible, but not its original "<u>Words</u>." Technically, Bible preservation has its primary meaning for the original Hebrew, Aramaic, and Greek "<u>Words</u>" and not in "*varying languages*."

No "Typos" In the Old Testament

STATEMENT #41: (pp. 25-26) "*It is obvious that Jesus did not consider the lack of the autographs an important matter, and he called the extant copies inspired in spite of any 'typos' in them.*"

COMMENT #41: These authors are saying that the Lord Jesus Christ believed, apparently, that there were "*typos*" or typographical errors or mistakes in the Old Testament. This is absolutely false. The Lord Jesus was the One Who gave those **Words** for the writers. He was the Logos or the Revelator and, as such, He gave every **Word** of the Hebrew Old Testament as well as every **Word** in the New Testament text to God the Holy Spirit. Then the Holy Spirit gave those **Words** to the writers to put down. God had preserved His "<u>Words</u>" until the time of the Lord Jesus Christ and there were no "*typos*."

STATEMENT #42: (p. 26) "*In all the passages regarding the <u>preservation</u> of the New Testament there is no direct statement regarding the <u>means</u> of it.*"

COMMENT #42: This is wrong. The '*<u>means</u>*' of preserving His New Testament is that He is going to preserve all the original **Words** of the New Testament. It is verbal "*<u>preservation</u>*". It is the "*<u>preservation</u>*" of the **Words**.

The Lord Jesus Christ mentioned this "*means*" in three different places in the New Testament (Matthew 24:35; Mark 13:31; and Luke 21:33). Each of these verses uses the identical Words both in the Greek and in the English King James Bible: "*Heaven and earth shall pass away, but my Words shall not pass away.*" The negative term used here is OU ME which is the strongest negative in the Greek language. It means the original Words of the Lord Jesus Christ shall never, never, never pass away. They will be preserved perfectly.

No "Inspired Writers"

STATEMENT #43: (p. 26) "*. . . in a manner similar to a supervision of the inspired writers themselves . . .*"

COMMENT #43: That is a gigantic error. I do not know what theology book these men were reading to have committed such gross theological error.

There are no such things as "*inspired writers.*" "*Inspired of God*" means "*God-breathed.*" God did not breathe out writers. The writers were moved, led, or carried along by the Holy Spirit according to 2 Peter 1:21: "*. . . Holy men of God spake as they were MOVED by the Holy Ghost.*" They were not "*inspired.*" They were "*moved.*"

The things that were "*given by inspiration of God*" were the original Words of the Old and New Testaments (2 Timothy 3:16). "*All Scripture* [PASA GRAPHE] *is given by inspiration of God...*"The words, PASA GRAPHE, refer to all which has been written down. It includes the Words and the letters that are "*God-breathed*" [THEOPNEUSTOS]. God breathed out the letters and Words, not the "*writers.*" This is a terrific error by these educated men on the staff of Bob Jones University.

"Sense" Not Enough

STATEMENT #44: (p. 27) "*Quotations of the sense rather than the letter do not jeopardize what is written in any way.*"

COMMENT #44: The "*sense*" is not enough. This shows once again the authors' satisfaction with only the "*ideas, thoughts, concepts, message, truth, or teachings,*" rather than the original Hebrew, Aramaic, and Greek "*Words*" of God. Bible preservation must apply to the original "*Words,*" not just the "*sense.*" This is heresy!

STATEMENT #45: (p. 27) "*According to Hills, since God chose special believers to inspire his Word in the first place (II Pet. 1:20-21), He must also have chosen special copyists to preserve that Word flawless.*"

COMMENT #45: These men do not believe in "*flawless*" preservation of God's original "*Words*" as Dr. Edward Hills believed. They are wrong in stating that "*special believers*" were chosen to "*inspire His Word.*" It was God Himself, not "*special believers,*" who "*inspired*" or breathed out His **Words**, not people. They merely wrote down what God breathed out or "*inspired.*"

STATEMENT #46: (p. 28) "*Those who reason this way do so to argue that the text of the New Testament, so providentially preserved in this fashion, is the Textus Receptus, as reflected in the majority of the manuscripts.*"

COMMENT #46: This is what I believe.

I believe that the original "**Words**" that God has preserved for us are the Hebrew, Aramaic, and Greek **Words** that underlie our King James Bible. These **Words** in the New Testament are called the **Textus Receptus** or the **Traditional Text**.

STATEMENT #47: (p. 28) "*They were but following the Lord's example, who had not been alarmed by variations in manuscripts during His earthly ministry.*"

COMMENT #47: This is a totally false and heretical position! These Bob Jones University men cannot point to one single place where our Lord Jesus Christ had any problem whatsoever with the Old Testament original "**Words**" as written and preserved down to His time! Where will this position of apostasy stop? The Lord Jesus Christ did not have any **variations** of **Words** in the Hebrew Old Testament manuscripts He held in His hands. The **Words** of the Old Testament Hebrew were preserved to the letter. The Lord Jesus Christ never found "*variations,*" and these writers cannot find any place where He believed this.

Phony "Preservation of Scripture"

STATEMENT #48: (p. 29) "*The correct view must not conflict with the promises of God concerning His preservation of Scripture . . .*"

COMMENT #48: When they use the expression "**preservation of "Scripture**," they do not mean the original Hebrew, Aramaic, and Greek "**Words**" of the Bible, but only the "*ideas, thoughts, concepts, message, truth, or teachings.*" This is a serious defect as will be shown further.

STATEMENT #49: (p. 30) "*Warfield also wrote an Introduction to Textual Criticism of the New Testament. In his work, he distinguishes purity of doctrinal content (substantial purity), from purity of transmission (textual purity).*"

COMMENT #49: Schnaiter and Tagliapietra agree with B. B. Warfield, a Westcott and Hort worshiper. They agree with this distinction. I do not agree with any such distinction. Just as Warfield before them, these two Bob Jones University staff men do not believe in "*textual purity*," but only "*substantial purity*," by which they mean that only the "*ideas, thoughts, concepts, message, truth, or teachings*" of the Bible have been preserved, but not its original "Words." This is a heretical and an apostate view and position. These men, and Bob Jones University that pays their salaries, believe there are "*textual*" errors and "typos" in the Hebrew, Aramaic, and Greek "Words".

STATEMENT #50: (p. 30) "*. . . they are not criticizing God's Word, but are criticizing a phrase which they believe to be one of those typos.*"

COMMENT #50: These men make provision for "*typos*" in the original Hebrew, Aramaic, and Greek Words. They are using the wrong Scriptures if they are looking at "*typos*." They should use the Hebrew, Aramaic, and Greek Words which underlie our King James Bible. There are no "*typos*" there. In their text there are all kinds of "*typos*," but none in the original "Words" that underlie our King James Bible.

STATEMENT #51: (p. 30) "*Though it may sound strange, it merely recognizes that a technical difference in sentence structure need not affect the message.*"

COMMENT #51: They do not care about "difference in sentence structure" so long as the "message" is there.

By "message" they show clearly that all they have in their view of "*Bible preservation*" is only the "*ideas, thoughts, concepts, message, truth, or teachings*," rather than the original Hebrew, Aramaic, and Greek "Words" of the Bible. I do not know why they call it Bible preservation. The Old and New Testaments of the Bible were made of original Hebrew, Aramaic, and Greek Words. Without preserving those original Words, there has been no genuine "*preservation*" of the "*Bible.*" It is very easy to understand.

New Testament "Sorely Corrupt"?

STATEMENT #52: (p. 30) "*With this in mind, Warfield gauges the 'purity' of the text of the New Testament by two measuring rods. First, he compares it to a modern book produced by modern proofreading methods, and with the original available for consultation. Compared to this the text of the New Testament is 'sorely corrupt.'*"

COMMENT #52: They are quoting this with approval. Do these two Bob Jones University staff members agree with this heretical and apostate position that "*the text of the New Testament is sorely corrupt*"? In the absence of a clear denial of this position, it appears that they agree with that false position. If this is the case, shame on these two authors and Bob Jones University for having them on their staff and holding to this position! This position is that of the apostates in the Roman Catholic Church, the apostates in the liberal modernistic churches, the compromisers in the neo-evangelical churches, and sadly many also who call themselves Fundamentalists.

STATEMENT #53: (p. 31) "*Warfield goes on to point out that the text of Scripture is substantially unaffected by the variations.*"

COMMENT #53: They do not completely divorce themselves from this statement that the text is "*substantially unaffected by the variations*," though it is in reality a "*deception.*"

> The text is affected in over 8,000 places. As I have mentioned before, Dr. Jack Moorman's 500-large-page research has catalogued over 8,000 differences between the Critical Text and the Text underlying our King James Bible (Cf. BFT #3084 @ $65.00 + $7.50 S&H).

Only "Competently Exact"?

STATEMENT #54: (p. 31) [Warfield's observations] "*. . . such has been the Providence of God in preserving for His church in each and every age a competently exact text of the Scriptures, . . . its comparatively infrequent blemishes . . . its wonderful approximation to its autographs.*"

COMMENT #54: In this quotation of Warfield with approval, the authors' true doubts in inerrant Bible preservation are shown clearly. The words "*competently exact,*" "*comparatively infrequent blemishes,*" and "*approximation to its autographs*" show plainly that these two Bob Jones University staff members, and therefore the University itself, denies perfect preservation of the original Hebrew, Aramaic, and Greek **Words** of our Bible. This is a heretical and an apostate position. It cannot be a true Fundamentalist position.

> Warfield was a pupil of Westcott and Hort and has had an influence on Schnaiter and his co-author.

STATEMENT #55: (p. 31) "*It is simply not true to say that the truth of Scripture is imperiled by textual impurities of the sort found in the New Testament manuscripts.*"

COMMENT #55: With the use of the words "*truth*" and "*textual impurities*," these authors clearly believe we do not have the original Hebrew, Aramaic, and Greek **Words** of the Bible preserved, but only the *"ideas, thoughts, concepts, message, truth, or teachings"* of that Bible. This is not *"Bible Preservation"* which is the title of their book. According to the study by Dr. Jack Moorman (BFT #3084), there are over 8,000 "*textual impurities*" in the Westcott and Hort/Nestle-Aland kind of text; but the original **Words** underlying our King James Bible do not have "*impurities*."

STATEMENT #56: (p. 31) [They quote Dr. David Otis Fuller] *"He says, 'THE BATTLE IS ON [emphasis his]' 'And Christian, the foundations of your faith and mine are now, this very moment under **bitter and vitriolic attack** by the enemy of our souls.'"*

COMMENT #56: Though these men no doubt take issue with Dr. Fuller's remarks as they do with Dr. Fuller's Hebrew, Aramaic, and Greek **Words** underlying the King James Bible, I agree with his statement. He was one of the Vice Presidents of our Dean Burgon Society until His death.

One of the most "**bitter and vitriolic attacks**" on our faith is found in the present book I am analyzing backed by the so-called "Citadel of the Faith" and of Fundamentalism, Bob Jones University in Greenville, South Carolina.

"Attacks" Not "Unsubstantiated"

STATEMENT #57: (p. 32) *". . . our air force pilots mistakenly bombed or fired upon our own troops and killed many of them. Spiritually, men like Fuller,* [that is David Otis Fuller] *well-intentioned as they may be, have nonetheless caused division and brought about spiritual casualties among God's people through such **indiscriminate and unsubstantiated attacks**."*

COMMENT #57: I do not believe Dr. David Otis Fuller made "*indiscriminate and unsubstantiated attacks*" on fellow Christians. I am right now, in this book, making "*substantiated attacks*" on Bob Jones University and its book by two of its staff members. The book you are now reading is loaded with facts. I am quoting the words of the authors right back at them. I am disputing them, arguing against them, and saying that their words, though from the pens of Fundamentalists, are false words, are modernistic words, and are non-Fundamentalist words in regard to the preservation of the Bible. I will continue to do so as long as Bob Jones University and its people keep on spouting such apostate and heretical positions on the Bible and its preservation!

"Controversy" Necessary

STATEMENT #58: (p. 32) *"This lure away from **clear Bible teachings** into **controversy** is second in seriousness only to doubts concerning inspiration caused by liberal critics such as Wellhausen."*

COMMENT #58: This *Bible Preservation* book is by no means "*clear Bible teachings.*" For this reason, I and others are correct in counteracting such falsehoods. This Schnaiter and Tagliapietra book follows, in the same falsehood train, as other Bob Jones University sponsored books like *From the **Mind** of God to the Mind of Man* (answered by my **BFT #2974 @ $7.00 + $3.00 S&H,** *Fundamentalist Mis-Information on Bible Versions*), and the most recent one, *God's **Word** in our Hands--the Bible Preserved for Us* (answered by my **BFT #3234 @ $8.00 + $3.00 S&H,** *Fundamentalist Deception on Bible Preservation*). These books abound in horrendous falsehoods, and no wonder we have to separate from that group. No wonder there must be division. No wonder there must be "*controversy,*" because truth is being besmirched by error, falsehood, and untruth. Those of us who stand for the truth must stand up against the falsehood, and this is what I am doing in my radio broadcasts by shortwave around the world and in books such as this one and the others mentioned above. I am analyzing this horrendous book on *Bible Preservation*, which is not preservation at all of the original Hebrew, Aramaic, and Greek **Words** of the Bible.

STATEMENT #59: (p. 32) "*In fact, we as authors do not hold the same view on the subject. But we invariably agree on the fundamental **teachings** of the **Word** of God, . . .*"

COMMENT #59: Notice their "*agreement*" is only on the "*teachings*" of the "**Word**" of God, by which they mean only the "*ideas, thoughts, concepts, message, truth, or teachings,*" but not the original Hebrew, Aramaic, and Greek **Words** of the Bible.

Not "Teachings of Men"

STATEMENT #60: (p. 32) "*. . . we hope that the artillery can be redirected against the **true enemies**: the army of **liberal theologians** who deny the **Word** of God and the snipers among us, **reactionaries that would divide this flock over these teachings of men**.*"

COMMENT #60: Here again "**Word**" is used, by which is meant only the "*ideas, thoughts, concepts, message, truth, or teachings*" of the Bible, but not its original Hebrew, Aramaic, and Greek "**Words**." These authors are saying that I am battling against the wrong "*enemies.*" I should go after the "*liberal theologians.*"

I am always going after the "*liberal theologians.*" I will continue to do so. But I will also continue to go after those Fundamentalists who are in accord with the "*liberal theologians*" when it comes to Bibliology including especially Bible preservation as in the case of these present authors and Bob Jones University who pays their salaries.

As Paul went after Peter for his falsities and *"withstood him to the face"* (Galatians 2:11b), so I will *"withstand"* these Bob Jones University men *"to their face."* They are wrong. They ought to be corrected. They are enemies of the truth in this area of theology. Not only are the *"liberal theologians"* enemies of the truth, but also Fundamentalists that deny this truth concerning the preservation of the original Hebrew, Aramaic, and Greek **Words** of the Bible. They are also enemies of the truth. I am not a *"sniper"* or a *"reactionary"* trying to divide the flock *"over the teachings of man."* These are the teachings of God--not of *"man."* As long as God gives me breath, I will fight FOR God's **Words** and truth and AGAINST any errors promulgated by all enemies of that truth (to paraphrase the loyalty oath to our U. S. Constitution) *"whether foreign* [liberals] *or domestic* [Fundamentalists in error]."

STATEMENT #61: (p. 32) *"We ask only that our statements be taken in context and not prejudged. May the Lord be glorified over His providence over His **Word**."*

COMMENT #61:   Here again "**Word**" is used, by which is meant only the *"ideas, thoughts, concepts, message, truth, or teachings"* of the Bible, but not its original Hebrew, Aramaic, and Greek "**Words**."

Only "Word" Not "Words"

STATEMENT #62:   (p. 33) [This is in the summary of the first chapter] *"The **inspiration** of Scripture is a clear doctrine of the Bible and includes the inerrancy of the infallible and authoritative* **[1]** ***Word** of God. The verbal and plenary inspiration of the Bible is the foundation of our faith. This raises the question of its **preservation**. It is clear that God has preserved His* **[2]** ***Word** .... God has promised to preserve His* **[3]** ***Word** in heaven forever."*

COMMENT #62: Notice the three uses of "**Word**." Do they use this term in the same way in all three uses? Remember, these authors and their school define "**Word**" as only *"ideas, thoughts, concepts, message, truth, or teachings"* but not God's original Hebrew, Aramaic, and Greek **Words**. If they use this term the same in all three cases, they have denied the *"inerrancy"* of the **Words** of God in "***inspiration***." This would be a serious heresy if this is the case. On the other hand, if they use "**Word**" for the original Hebrew, Aramaic, and Greek "**Words**" in the first use, and then use "**Word**" in their usual sense of merely the *"ideas, thoughts, concepts, message, truth, or teachings,"* but not the original **Words**, they are using clever deception in their use of terminology and redefinition of this term in the same context, using one meaning for "***inspiration***" and another meaning for "***preservation***."

STATEMENT #63:   (p. 33) *"Though the Bible describes a little of the process of **inspiration**, it does not describe in detail the process of **preservation**. Since God also chose, in his Providence, **not to preserve the***

autographs, it takes more effort to understand the process."
    COMMENT #63: God has "*preserved the autographs*" in the exact APOGRAPHS or copies of the Hebrew, Aramaic, and Greek <u>Words</u> underlying our King James Bible.

> The authors of this book do not believe that we have any preserved autographs. They don't know where the <u>Words</u> of God are. In other words, these men do not know where the original Hebrew, Aramaic, and Greek <u>Words</u> of the Bible are. All they have is some "*ideas, thoughts, concepts, message, truth, or teachings,*" but not the original <u>Words</u>.

Warfield Not A Good Defender

STATEMENT #64: (p. 34) [Under the section on Questions] "*Who wrote the greatest defense of Scripture ever penned, The Inspiration and Authority of the Bible?*"
    COMMENT #64: The authors' answer to the question is B. B. Warfield. But, in reality, that work is NOT the "*greatest defense of Scripture ever penned.*" It follows the false critical Greek text of Westcott and Hort. It is also weak and false on the Bible preservation of the original Hebrew, Aramaic, and Greek <u>Words</u> of the Bible.

STATEMENT #65: (p. 34) [Again a question] "*Describe the twin dangers for the students of the Bible regarding the preservation of the Bible?*"
    COMMENT #65: Certainly these authors do not have a proper belief regarding the "*preservation of the Bible.*" They do not believe in the preservation of the original Hebrew, Aramaic, and Greek <u>Words</u> of the Bible. To these writers, that would be one of the real dangers, though I would disagree with them on this.

CHAPTER 2

PRESERVED SINCE ANTIQUITY

"Homer" Not "Classical Greek"

STATEMENT #66: (p. 37) [This is in Chapter Two, "Preserved since Antiquity"] "*Interestingly, though, until the late 1800's, it was thought that the New Testament was written in classical Greek just like Homer.*"
    COMMENT #66: This is a statement made from ignorance on the part of these two erudite, intelligent, and well-trained authors. Did they learn this nonsense at Bob Jones University?

The Greek of <u>Homer</u> is not called "*classical Greek*." It is called "Homeric Greek" from a much older period of the Greek language. It has its own peculiar grammar. It is found in works such as Homer's *The Iliad* and *The Odyssey*, which we read when I majored in Classical Greek and Latin at the University of Michigan, 1945--1948 under the direction of Dr. Warren E. Blake, the head of the Classics Department. Classical Greek, on the other hand, has a variety of styles, whether Ionic, Doric, or Attic. That is the Greek used by Plato and Aristotle. It has a completely different grammar, vocabulary, and style.

CHAPTER 3
PRESERVATION IN QUANTITY

STATEMENT #67: (p. 46) "*. . . the fact that the* [Old Testament] *scribes called Masoretes even counted letters to insure accurate copying gave Christians a basis from which to argue preservation of this Masoretic Text. However, the Higher Critics simply scoffed.*"

COMMENT #67: There certainly is every reason to believe in the accurate "*preservation*" of the original Masoretic Hebrew <u>Words</u> underlying our King James Old Testament.

Yes, *the Higher Critics simply scoffed*, but so do these authors, Bob Jones University that pays their salaries, and many other Fundamentalists around the world. Sad to say, it is not only the "*Higher Critics*" that deny the accurate "*preservation*" of the Old Testament Hebrew and Aramaic <u>Words</u>.

"Erasmus" Not the "Basis" for KJB

STATEMENT #68: (p. 49) "*Erasmus, who prepared the first Greek New Testament published on a printing press, depended upon this manuscript* [Codex 2] *for the Gospels, only occasionally making changes based on another manuscript. That printing eventually became the basis for our beloved King James Version.*"

COMMENT #68:

While it is true that Erasmus "*prepared the first Greek New Testament published on a printing press,*" it is totally false that this was the "*basis for our beloved King James Version.*"

That last part is as false as the day is long. When are these learned scholars of Bob Jones University, Detroit Baptist Seminary, Central Baptist Seminary, Calvary Baptist Seminary, Maranatha Baptist Bible College, Northland Baptist Bible College, and others going to stop making the horrendous error about the "*basis*" for the King James Bible?

The way they treat the King James Bible, why do they call it "*beloved*"? When they sell and permit the use of other English versions which are "*beloved*" to them, how can they still call the King James Bible "*beloved*"? Among those who are married, having two or more "*beloveds*" would be called adultery. In this case, it might be called versional adultery.

> **The truth of the matter is that our King James Bible was not based on Erasmus' Greek of 1516, but upon Beza's 5th Edition, 1598, eighty-two years later.**

Will these Critical Text schools ever own up to the truth of this matter? I should hope so. These schools have repeatedly uttered this blatant falsehood despite the many times in my various books I have attempted to straighten them out with the truth.

No Manuscript "Families"

STATEMENT # 69: (pp. 49-50) *"There are also a few families of manuscripts among the minuscules. A family is named when some scholar groups together a number of manuscripts having distinctive similarities that he deems important."*

COMMENT #69:

> **I do not believe in the "*family*" theory first propounded by Westcott and Hort in the *Introduction* to their 1881 Greek text. Neither Dean John W. Burgon, nor Edward Miller, nor Dr. Frederick Scrivener believed in "*families*" either.**

Dean Burgon said that the New Testament manuscripts are simply like orphan children with little or no relation one to another. He said that perhaps there are one or two where you can find that this one was derived from another one, but that was all. He said it would be just like going into a cemetery with unmarked graves. The people buried there had died hundreds of years before. That is exactly what we have with the Greek New Testament manuscripts. The manuscripts are not broken up into "*families*." They are like orphan children.

"Preserving" Only "His Word"

STATEMENT #70: (p. 52) *". . . the New Testament is more than eight to one than the next most frequent book. Such evidence proves that God* *has fulfilled his <u>promise to preserve His Word.</u>"*

COMMENT #70:   Here again they are referring to God's "<u>promise to preserve His Word</u>" instead of the preservation of God's "<u>Words</u>." By this term they believe that God has preserved only His "*ideas, thoughts, concepts, message, truth, or teachings,*" rather than the original Hebrew, Aramaic, and Greek <u>Words</u>. This is deceptively dishonest.

CHAPTER 4
PRESERVATION
THROUGH DISSEMINATION
"Origen" Not A Defender

STATEMENT #71:   (p. 56) [From Chapter 4, "Preservation Through Dissemination"] *"By the middle of the third century, five other important fathers had also died: Origen and Clement of Alexandria, Hippolytus of Rome, Tertulian and Cyprian of Carthage. Of these, Origen is the most famous. His <u>defense of Christianity</u> from the first serious attacks of secular philosophy (Celsus) bring him credit.   However, . . . he sets a <u>wrong example</u> for hermeneutics (interpretation)."*

COMMENT #71:   It is true Origen's false hermeneutics is a "<u>wrong example</u>," but I would not say that Origen had a "<u>defense of Christianity</u>."   He was one of the leading Gnostic heretics of Alexandria following Clement.   His bad life example and false doctrines are not to be commended by anyone.   He certainly had perverse New Testament manuscripts that he continued to doctor for the worse.

STATEMENT #72:   (p. 64)   *"The first <u>Greek translation</u> of the Pentateuch (five books of Moses) was made by Jews at Alexandria during the reign of Ptolemy Philadelphus <u>258-246 B.C.</u>"*

COMMENT #72:   That is a false statement without documentary proof of any kind. It merely parrots the report of the apocryphal and fanciful *Letter of Aristeas.*

> There are no B.C. copies of the entire Pentateuch in Greek.   They cannot prove that the Pentateuch was B.C., much less the entire Old Testament from Genesis through Malachi, which is also wrongly thought to be made B.C.   The Septuagint Greek Old Testament was made in the 200's A.D. by Origen of Alexandria and was placed in the fifth column of his Hexapla Bible.

"Septuagint" Not Quoted By Jesus

STATEMENT #73: (p. 65) *"The Septuagint like any other version, is not a perfect translation of the Hebrew. The amazing thing is that both Jesus and Paul quoted it."*

> **COMMENT #73:** There is no clear documentary proof of this. It is a false statement.

> **Neither Jesus nor Paul quoted** from the *"Septuagint"* which was not even in existence in their day. It was a product of the 200's A.D. in the era of Origen.

The *"Septuagint"* was the 5th column of Origen's HEXAPLA. If anything was the case, the *"Septuagint"* quoted the words of Jesus and Paul. As I mentioned in the former page, the *Letter of Aristeas* is that apocryphal book where they try to say that 70 Jews translated the first five books of the Bible in 70 days. That *Letter of Aristeus* is little more than a fairy tale and these authors should know better than to take these lies as the Gospel truth.

STATEMENT #74: (pp. 66-67) *"Either way, this quotation of the Greek is just as inspired as the Hebrew original, so neither should be accused of error. . . . None of this requires that the Septuagint was inspired in the same way that the Hebrew was . . . ."*

> **COMMENT #74:** It sounds like these authors believe the *"Septuagint"* to be "inspired." If so, they have a desperately flawed understanding of what *"inspired"* means in the Bible. The New Testament uses it in relation to the original **Words** in 2 Timothy 3:16. *"Given by inspiration of God"* is the translation of the one Greek Word THEOPNEUSTOS. This word comes from two Greek **Words**, THEOS [God] and PNEUSTOS. PNEUSTOS comes from the verb PNEO which means *"to breathe."* The resultant meaning is *"God-breathed."*

> These authors are wrong stating that both the Hebrew **Words** and the translated Greek **Words** of the Old Testament Septuagint were *"God-breathed."* This is a fatal error and is a serious heresy! Only the Hebrew, Aramaic, and Greek **Words** were *"God-breathed."* By their putting on a par both the Hebrew and a translation of that Hebrew is a serious theological heresy of Bibliology.

It ill-behooves Bob Jones University and its staff members to permit such a fuzzy view of Biblical inspiration. The issue is not whether or not the *"inspiration"* is the same in Hebrew versus a translation. The fact is there is no *"inspiration"* whatsoever in that translation or any other translation.

> God did not breathe out translations, only His original Hebrew, Aramaic, and Greek Words.

STATEMENT #75:   (p. 67)   *"Neither Jesus nor the apostles worshiped a specific manuscript or translation of the Old Testament. The autographs were long gone and they did not fret over it, nor doubt whether they had God's Word. They trusted God's Word in the languages of the day so fully, that 'it is written' settled the issue."*

COMMENT #75: Notice that here again these authors talk about *"God's Word in the languages of the day."* This cannot be a reference to God's *"Words,"* but only God's *"Word,"* by which they mean only His *"ideas, thoughts, concepts, message, truth, or teachings,"* rather than the original Hebrew, Aramaic, and Greek *Words*. This is deceptively dishonest. God's *"ideas, thoughts, concepts, message, truth, or teachings"* might be *"in the languages of the day,"* but only the original Hebrew, Aramaic, and Greek *Words* constitute the true Bible. I would have expected staff members and teachers of Bob Jones University to have been crystal clear on these important points. But there is obscurity, obfuscation, and confusion here. God is not the author of confusion (1 Corinthians 14:33).

The Ruckman Position Taken

STATEMENT #76:   (p. 67)   *"They did not tolerate deliberate tampering with Scripture either. Peter said that men did so 'to their own destruction.' Yet versions that honestly attempted to translate (rather than tamper) were accepted as the inspired Word of God."*

COMMENT #76: How errant can these authors get? They are again promulgating heretical teaching and apostate doctrine. They are saying wrongfully that *"versions"* (that is, translations) are *"the inspired Word of God."* Nothing could be further from the truth.

> *"Versions"* are not breathed out by God, hence they can never properly and Scripturally be referred to as *"inspired."* Every translation in whatever language, based on whatever Hebrew, Aramaic, and Greek foundation, and however accurate they are, they are still the work of men, not the work of God Himself.

This applies to English translations (including the King James Bible), French translations, Spanish translations, or any other language translation. They are not *"God-breathed,"* hence they are not *"inspired."* Where is the Scriptural proof by these writers that God breathed out any of these translations?

> In saying that translations are "*inspired*," these writers have taken the position of Peter Ruckman who says that the King James Bible translation is "*inspired*."

In this agreement with Ruckman on this point, these writers (and even Bob Jones University who pays their salaries) could be called Ruckmanites. I am sure they would not want this epithet. If they do not, they should change their erroneous position on "*inspired*" translations.

Here again these authors are referring to God's "**Word**" instead of God's "**Words**." By this term they believe that God has preserved only His "*ideas, thoughts, concepts, message, truth, or teachings*," rather than the original Hebrew, Aramaic, and Greek **Words**. This is deceptively dishonest and defective.

More "Ruckmanism"

STATEMENT #77: (p. 67) "*With these facts in mind, we need never to be ashamed to hold up __an English Bible__ and declare 'This is the __inspired Word of God__.'*"

COMMENT #77: The authors do not even specify which English Bible they are speaking of. They would include the New International Version, a New American Standard Version, the English Standard Version, the Revised Standard Version, the New Revised Standard Version, the Contemporary English Version, or any other so-called "__English Bible__." I cannot hold up any of those versions and say they are the "__inspired Word of God__."

> "__Inspired__" is a word that must have God as the subject of it. God "__inspired__" or breathed out only the **Words** of Hebrew, Aramaic, and Greek. He did not breathe out translations. Again, their position is a false Ruckmanite position in this area of "__inspired__" translations.

STATEMENT #78: (p. 67) "*Christians should rejoice when the inspired __Word__ of God is translated into each language. More will be said about versions in a later chapter. For now, it is enough to note that God has __preserved His Word in many versions__ for the purpose of spreading the Gospel 'to every people, nation, language, and tongue.'*"

COMMENT #78: Here again these authors are referring to God's "**Word**" instead of God's "**Words**." By this term they believe that God has preserved only His "*ideas, thoughts, concepts, message, truth, or teachings*" rather than the original Hebrew, Aramaic, and Greek **Words**. This is deceptively dishonest and defective. Capital "P" Preservation is referred to in Psalm 12:6-7:

> [6]*The Words of the LORD* are pure **Words**: as silver tried in a furnace of earth, purified seven times. [7] Thou shalt keep them, O LORD, **thou shalt preserve them** from this generation for ever.

It is the Preservation God has promised for His original Hebrew, Aramaic, and Greek **Words**. No translation of the Bible partakes of this kind of Preservation which is reserved for the original **Words**.

I use a small "p" preservation when those Preserved Hebrew, Aramaic, and Greek **Words** are accurately and faithfully translated into the words of various languages of the world such as has been done in the King James Bible. In that sense, these translations "*preserve*" (with a small "p") the Hebrew, Aramaic, and Greek **Words** as they translate these **Words** into the language in question. This is what the translators of the King James Bible have done.

> **Because of this I believe that the King James Bible preserves the original Preserved Hebrew, Aramaic, and Greek Words by translating them accurately into the English language. I believe that in the King James Bible we have God's Words kept intact in English.**

Statements on Unit II Transmission of Scripture

Preserved "Word" not "Words"

STATEMENT #79: (p. 71) *"You have seen that God has <u>preserved</u> <u>His</u> <u>Word.</u> The issues among Christians involve the manner in which He did so."* **COMMENT #79:** Here again these authors are referring to God's "<u>Word</u>" instead of God's "<u>Words</u>." By this term they believe that God has preserved only His *"ideas, thoughts, concepts, message, truth, or teachings,"* rather than the original Hebrew, Aramaic, and Greek <u>Words</u>. This is deceptively dishonest and defective. These Bob Jones University staff men do not believe that God has preserved His original Hebrew, Aramaic, and Greek <u>Words</u>. I disagree completely with Bob Jones University's heretical and apostate Bibliology, or doctrine of the Bible.

CHAPTER 5
THE HISTORY OF THE TRANSMISSION THEORIES
Was the "Vulgate" Inspired?

STATEMENT #80: (p. 77) [regarding 1 John 5:7-8] *"Both sides accused the other of tampering with sacred Scripture. Catholics believe that Erasmus was removing <u>Words</u> from Scripture based on the <u>inspired Vulgate</u> while Erasmus argued from the Greek that the Catholics had already added to the Bible."*

COMMENT #80: The way these Bob Jones University writers have written this sentence, it might indicate that they believe there is such a thing as an *"<u>inspired Vulgate</u>."* They do not qualify that sentence. They could have made it clear by saying "... *<u>based on what they believed to be an</u> <u>inspired Vulgate</u>.*" But they did not.

Are these authors agreeing that their false concept of *"<u>inspiration</u>"* extends even to the Latin *"<u>Vulgate</u>?"*

I certainly hope that these authors do not believe that the Vulgate was "*inspired*" or God-breathed. Their words as they stand could be construed in that way.

What Kind of a "Humanist"?

STATEMENT #81: (p. 80) "*Erasmus, though more a humanist than a Christian, made several key contributions to the study of manuscripts.*"

COMMENT #81: The authors are doing two things regarding Erasmus: (1) They are demeaning him as a "*Christian.*" Though I do not know his heart beliefs or lack thereof, Erasmus certainly wanted everyone to read the Bible for themselves. That is certainly a Christian virtue. (2) They are smearing him as a "*humanist*" without defining what they mean by that term. They are using the current meaning of "*humanist*" to designate an atheistic person. That was not the position of Erasmus. He was a humanitarian who believed in helping people, he was by no means an atheist as the modern "*humanists.*" They are doing both things because they do not like the Greek text of which he published and printed.

> These authors teach falsely that the Erasmus Text was the basis of the King James Bible. It was Beza's 5th Edition 1598 that was the basis of the King James Bible. This was eighty-two years after the 1516 Edition of Erasmus.

"Received Text" Not "Erasmus"

STATEMENT #82: (p. 80) "*The phrase Received Text or Textus Receptus (in Latin) traces to this preface that has come to refer to the Greek Text of Erasmus.*"

COMMENT #82: This is a reference to the 1633 Elzevir Brothers Greek New Testament. They were from Holland. The reference was in Latin which referred to "*a text which was received by all.*"

> The implication is that this "*Received Text*" or "*Textus Receptus*" began either with the Elzevir text or that of Erasmus in 1516, both of which implications are totally false. The "*Received Text*" was a group of manuscripts which originated from the original Greek Words of the apostles Peter, Paul, James, John and the original writers. This is a serious error.

These men of Bob Jones University have been trained and taught wrong in this area of the "*Textus Receptus*" and the "*Received Text*," and have been teaching this error at that school with the full approval of the leaders of that institution.

STATEMENT #83: (p. 83) *"Since modern textual criticism stresses* <u>*scribal habits, genealogy, text types, and the oldest manuscripts*</u> *Bengel is rightly considered 'the father of modern New Testament textual criticism.'"*

COMMENT #83: Bengel and these writers are wrong on the subject of "<u>*scribal habits, genealogy, text types, and the oldest manuscripts*</u>." All of their views on these topics are corrupt and flawed.

8,000 Words in Doubt for Them

STATEMENT #84: (p. 83) *"Scholars of every conceivable position acknowledge that seven out of every eight verses in the New Testament have no textual problems. In other words 87% of the* <u>*Words*</u> *of Scripture are not in doubt no matter what manuscript or groups of manuscripts you think is the best."*

COMMENT #84: This percentage is only a guess. It is a quotation from heretics Westcott and Hort as mentioned in their *Introduction* to their 1881 Greek New Testament text. This gives the appearance that there are very few differences between the Critical Text and the Received Text. As I have mentioned before, Dr. Jack Moorman's 500-large-page research has catalogued **over 8,000 differences** between the Critical Text and the Text underlying our King James Bible (Cf. BFT #3084 @ $65.00 + $7.50 S&H). The statistics of these writers are deceptive and false.

"Meaning" and "Doctrine" Affected

STATEMENT #85: (p. 83) *"None of these* <u>*variants*</u> *affect* <u>*meaning*</u> *much less* <u>*doctrine*</u>."

COMMENT #85: This is absolutely and totally false. The differences in both "<u>*meaning*</u>" and "<u>*doctrine*</u>" found in the false Westcott and Hort type of text used at Bob Jones University are numerous. You can call it the Nestle/Aland Text or the United Bible Societies Text if you wish, but it is basically the same text of "B" and "Aleph" the Vatican and Sinai.

> To say there are no "<u>*variants*</u>" in "<u>*meaning*</u>" is obviously false. In the New Testament, Dr. Jack Moorman has outlined <u>over 8,000 differences</u> between the Greek Text of Nestle/Aland and the Greek Text underlying the King James Bible. It is a result of hundreds of hours of research. It gives the Greek words and the English translations.

This book of over 500-large-pages on *"8,000 Differences between the NIV and Modern Versions and the Words Underlying the King James Bible"* is available from the BIBLE FOR TODAY for a gift of **$65.00 + $7.50 S&H**. It is BFT #3084. It is true that many of these differences do not affect meaning, but there are many that do affect it.

Once again I invite the reader to get a copy and study Dr. Jack Moorman's 100-large-page documentation on *356 Doctrinal Passages in the NIV and Its Underlying Greek Text* **(BFT #2956 @ $10 + $4 S&H)**. These come mainly from the Westcott and Hort type of text. The English translations based on these false words are therefore incorrect in "*doctrine*."

Where were these writers born? What have they been reading? To whom have they been listening? Why have they missed these 356 doctrinal passages? The fact is that these Bob Jones University staff members simply have not even analyzed the subject, nor looked into it as Dr. Jack Moorman of London, England has done. If you are interested in either of Dr. Jack Mormon's books call The BIBLE FOR TODAY at **1-800-John 10:9** and ask how to get them.

STATEMENT #86: (p. 84) "*This means that 99.9% of the Greek New Testament is free from variants that significantly affect meaning*."

COMMENT #86: This is absolutely false. These writers are just quoting heretics Westcott and Hort's *Introduction*. That is not the way it is. Can you explain to me or these two Bob Jones University men how they can squeeze **over 8,000 differences** (many of which "*affect meaning*") into 1/10th of 1% of space in the Greek New Testament? This is impossible!

STATEMENT #87: (p. 84) "*The most important conclusion is that even those few variants that affect meaning do not affect doctrine*."

COMMENT #87: May I repeat myself and say that this is totally false? How could these men write such a falsehood? Are these men asleep? Once again I invite the reader to get a copy and study Dr. Jack Moorman's 100-large-page documentation on *356 Doctrinal Passages in the NIV and Its Underlying Greek Text* **(BFT #2956 @ $10 + $4 S&H)**. These passages are found in their favorite Vatican and Sinai Critical Text to see how large a lie they have just written.

STATEMENT #88: (p. 84) "*It cannot be stressed too heavily that not one textual variant affects even one single teaching of Scripture. Fully 100% of the Greek New Testament is free from variants that alter doctrine*."

COMMENT #88: When are they going to stop these lies and falsehoods? Do you see why I attack the teachings and views of these brethren which are filled with such errors and falsehoods? I again invite the reader to get a copy and study Dr. Jack Moorman's 100-large-page documentation on *356 Doctrinal Passages in the NIV and Its Underlying Greek Text* **(BFT #2956 @ $10 + $4 S&H)**. Mark it well. These writers and Bob Jones University that employs them are in serious error on this false statement. I am not attacking their person but their ideas, views and teachings. Do you see why I attack the false views and position of Bob Jones University? It is because they are to be blamed.

> Christians who do not think that doctrine is involved in the false New Testament text that is used at Bob Jones University and their fellow-schools are on the wrong footing.

This is deception, dishonesty, and falsehood. I am glad I have broadcast these words over a worldwide audience by means of two powerful shortwave stations. Everybody in this hemisphere, in Europe, and in Asia can hear my voice every single week. I am telling the world not to trust Bob Jones University for anything in regard to the Bible texts, Bible versions, or Bible preservation. They should certainly not listen to the lies that these two Bob Jones University staff members have perpetrated by saying that "*doctrine*" is not affected. These men are uninformed, misinformed, and are misinforming others. Those who are writing books about this subject and do not know what they are talking about should stop writing books.

Only "Integrity" But Not "Words"?

STATEMENT #89: (p. 84) "*God has preserved the integrity of His Word and everyone who studies the issue recognizes this fact.*"

COMMENT #89: Here again these authors are referring to God's "Word" instead of God's "Words." By the phrase "*preserved the integrity of His Word*" these writers believe that God has preserved only His "*ideas, thoughts, concepts, message, truth, or teachings,*" rather than the original Hebrew, Aramaic, and Greek Words. It is a false view of Bible preservation.

STATEMENT #90: (p. 87) "*Westcott and Hort used Bengel's genealogical method to group the manuscripts. They found four text types, three of which had been previously identified by Bengel and Griesbach. Besides the Western Type identified by Griesbach, they identified both an Assyrian and an Alexandrian Text Type corresponding to Bengel's Asiatic and African types.*"

COMMENT #90: We are in the section of their book, which talks about B.F. Westcott (1825-1901) and F. J. A. Hort (1828-1892). I do not believe in "*text types*."

> As Dean Burgon said, all the manuscripts are like orphan children, without any known parents. He said it was just like people visiting a graveyard with 5,000 unmarked graves. There would be no way that people could identify the relatives of anyone in the cemetery. There is no such thing as "*text types.*"

This is a figment of Westcott and Hort's imagination to put over on the Christian world their false trust in the Vatican ("B") and the Sinai ("Aleph") manuscripts.

No "Conflation"

STATEMENT #91:   (p. 88) *"They termed this __conflation__, and claimed that this meant that the conflate reading must be more recent than the two that had been combined."*

COMMENT #91:

Our answer to that is this: there is no such thing as "*__conflation__*." Westcott and Hort gave a very small number of alleged "*__conflations__*."

Only one or two examples out of the eight that are mentioned by Westcott and Hort can even pretend to meet the terms of their alleged "*__conflations__*." In reality the original wording was AB. The heretics removed either A or B. Westcott and Hort had the order reversed. A + B did not equal AB, but AB was there first and A or B was split off from the original.   Their ideas of "*__conflation__*" are false.

Early Church Fathers Had the TR

STATEMENT #92:   (p. 88) *"Second, they* [that is, Westcott and Hort] *pointed out that __Syrian readings__ are never found __quoted by the church fathers__ before A.D. 350, a clear evidence of late text."*

COMMENT #92: This statement is completely false. Dean Burgon proved this to be false in his book, *The Traditional Text of the Holy Gospels* (BFT #1159 @ $15.00 + $5 S&H). [A summary of the evidence is found in BFT #2428 @ $3.50 + $2 S&H.]

> In that book, Dean Burgon assembled seventy-six early church fathers that died 400 AD or before. Many of these lived before 350 AD where Westcott and Hort said that there was no trace of any Traditional Text or Textus Receptus Words.

Dean Burgon and his research team found the Traditional Text readings were not only found, but in a ratio of three to two (60% to 40%). Dr. Jack Moorman, who is a missionary in London, England, has made a similar study and found the ratio of Traditional Text to the false Critical Text to be 70% to 30% in favor of the Traditional Text (Cf. **BFT #2428 @ $3.50+$3.00 S&H**). These men had the Received Text in their hands in those early days of 350 AD.

No "Recension" of Greek TR

STATEMENT #93:   (p. 88) *"They postulated that the vast number of manuscripts exhibiting such obviously late readings must be due to a __recension__, that is an official addition of the Bible such as that made by Jerome."*

COMMENT #93: I do not believe in a "*__recension__*" or a special edition. Westcott and Hort tried their best to explain away why so many manuscripts were identical to each other. So they invented a "*recension.*"

> This is a fairy tale. They tell the lie that all the leaders of the churches in 250 A.D. and then again in 350 A.D. brought all their manuscripts together and threw out all of the Vatican and Sinai ("B" and "Aleph") manuscripts and kept only those that followed the Traditional Text or the Textus Receptus. That is what they called a "*recension.*"

The lie goes on to say that from that point in history (250 or 350 A.D.) and afterwards, they just had copies of that "*recension*" or special edition. This is absolutely false. If this had happened, it would have been such a magnificent and gigantic event in the churches history there would have been some historical analysis of it. But there is not a single mention of it in any history book in the world. It did not take place.

Dean Burgon said that even if there had been a "*recension*" in 250 or 350 A.D. (and there was not), that would have been the best thing in the world. That would have meant that these early leaders would have brought very early copies of the Bible, including probably even some of the originals, to such a meeting. They would have thrown out into the garbage all of those false manuscripts that agreed with the Vatican and Sinai ("B" and "Aleph") manuscripts. This would include the Critical Text, the Nestle-Aland Text, the Westcott and Hort Text, and the United Bible Society Text. The only problem is that there was no such thing as a "*recension*" that was made. The true explanation as to why so many manuscripts were the same is that they were accurate copies of the originals themselves which refute the Critical Text.

"Genealogy" of MSS Is Erroneous

STATEMENT #94: (p. 88) "*They obviously depended upon the work of Bengel and Griesbach for the concept of genealogy, text type, and canons of scribal tendency.*"

COMMENT #94: As mentioned before, I do not accept the approach of either "*genealogy*" or "*text types.*" This is the false theory that one Bible manuscript was taken from another and then another and another. They say it was a type of text that came down from a family tree. Such is not the case as Dean Burgon has pointed out. Each manuscript is like an orphaned child with no ability to say where it came from. It is like Burgon's illustration of the cemetery which had unmarked graves. There is no proof that the person in one grave was related to people in any of the other graves.

Recent Editions Close to W&H

STATEMENT #95: (p. 89) "*. . . the insight and judgment that they applied to textual research has ruled the field of textual thinking from their day*" *to the present. . . . Even the most recent editions of the Greek New Testament are substantially based on Westcott and Hort's Greek text.*"

COMMENT #95: I agree with this statement, but disagree that their "*insight and judgment*" was worthwhile and correct. It is the wrong emphasis. It is the wrong basis. It is the wrong thinking. I am glad that these writers admit that "*all the modern editions of the Greek New Testament are substantially based on Westcott and Hort's Greek Text.*"

STATEMENT #96: (p. 89) "*. . . the application of sound critical research principles.*"

COMMENT #96: There indeed must be proper "*principles*," but Westcott and Hort had improper "*principles*." Dean Burgon had proper standards to determine the proper text of Scripture. His books are found on the Dean Burgon Society Website (**http://www.deanburgonsociety. org/idx_dbspress. htm**).

STATEMENT #97: (p. 89) "*The Westcott-Hort Text has thus effectively replaced the one Desiderius Erasmus edited in 1516-22.*"

COMMENT #97: That may be true, but that is not the text that was "*replaced*." There were several Greek New Testament texts which "*replaced*" the Erasmus text, including Stephens, Complutensian Polyglot, Beza, and Elzevir.

> What they should say is that the "*Westcott and Hort Text*" has replaced Beza's 5th edition 1598 on which the King James Bible was based.

STATEMENT #98: (p. 90) [They write about John W. Burgon's (1813-1888) and his critiques] "*Burgon attacked the genealogical foundation of the theory of Westcott and Hort and exposed some unproven assumptions. While the principle of genealogy cannot be disputed (since manuscripts were certainly copied from earlier manuscripts), no existing manuscript has been shown to be a direct copy of another existing manuscript.*"

COMMENT #98: This explains Dean Burgon's refutation of the false "*genealogical foundation*" of the theory of Westcott and Hort which is also held by these writers.

> All manuscripts are like orphan children and like unmarked graves. It cannot be conclusively shown that one manuscript was related to another.

STATEMENT #99: (p. 92) [Referring to Dean Burgon's view on Bible preservation] "*Burgon's reference to the Greek text underlying the KJV as the 'Traditional Text' is due to his view of it's preservation. He conceived of the text as handed down from God to the Church and by the Church handed* *down through the ages by tradition."*

COMMENT #99: With Burgon, I believe this Traditional Text was given by God the Holy Spirit and handed down to the churches and by the churches. There is nothing wrong with Burgon's statement of textual "*preservation*." These writers are trying to make arguments against the Traditional Text. The <u>Words</u> underlying our King James Bible are the <u>Words</u>, I believe, God has preserved for us according to His promise.

"Heretics" Did "Mutilate" the N.T.

STATEMENT #100: (pp. 92-93) "*. . . Burgon refers instead to readings here and there which differ in wording among the manuscripts from what he considers the true text of the New Testament. He reckons these as so mutilated by heretics that no conscientious Christian could conceivably have anything to do with them.*"

COMMENT #100: That is exactly what Dean Burgon does with "B" and "Aleph"--the Vatican and Sinai manuscripts. These writers and Bob Jones University that employs them disagree with Dean Burgon and hold these "*mutilated*" manuscripts to be the true ones.

STATEMENT #101: (p. 93) "*One estimate is that even the nearest two manuscripts (members of the <u>Majority text</u>) vary from each other as many as six to ten times per chapter.*" [I suppose that means either the Majority text of Hodges and Farstad or the Textus Receptus]."

COMMENT #101: They do not define what they mean by "*Majority Text*." Sometimes this refers to the Textus Receptus and at other times the text of Hodges and Farstad or Robertson and Pierpont texts. The Textus Receptus manuscripts vary in spellings somewhat. Let them vary.

I believe that God has preserved his Hebrew, Aramaic, and Greek <u>Words</u> that underlie our King James Bible. That is what He has preserved. That is Bible preservation.

As far as using the estimate of six to ten times per chapter, I do not accept it to be true. I have not checked it out myself. Even if it were true, it is not that great a number of spelling differences. Their manuscripts of "B" and "Aleph" have many more than that.

God's "Words" Not "Undisturbed"

STATEMENT #102: (p. 93) "*As regards these wording <u>differences</u>, the church down through the ages has reasonably concluded that <u>God's Word</u> remains <u>undisturbed</u> in spite of those <u>minor wording variants</u>.*"

COMMENT #102: Notice that here again these authors are referring to God's "<u>Word</u>" instead of God's "<u>Words</u>." By this term they believe that God has preserved only His "*ideas, thoughts, concepts, message, truth, or teachings,*" rather than the original Hebrew, Aramaic, and Greek <u>Words</u>. They believe that "*<u>God's Word</u>*" is "*<u>undisturbed</u>*" despite "*<u>wording differences</u>*." They could not refer to the preservation of God's <u>Words</u> which could have no "*<u>word differences</u>*." I believe there is one true text, and we really believe that the text and its Hebrew, Aramaic, and Greek <u>Words</u> which underlie our King James Bible, are the preserved <u>Words</u> of the living God. Our King James Bible is the only accurate translation of those preserved Hebrew, Aramaic, and Greek <u>Words</u>.

STATEMENT #103: (p. 94) "*That is to say , as far as satisfying the promises and integrity of God, and the authority and inerrancy of His <u>Word</u> is concerned, the variants leave <u>these matters largely undisturbed</u>.*"

COMMENT #103: "*<u>These matters</u>*" being "*<u>largely undisturbed</u>*" refer only to God's "<u>Word</u>" instead of God's "<u>Words</u>." By this term they believe that God has preserved only His "*ideas, thoughts, concepts, message, truth, or teachings,*" rather than the original Hebrew, Aramaic, and Greek <u>Words</u>. On the contrary, if they are referring to the "<u>Words</u>" of God, the false Greek texts and the false modern versions do not leave those "<u>Words</u>" "*largely undisturbed.*" As I have mentioned before, Dr. Jack Moorman's 500-large-page research has catalogued **over 8,000 differences** between the Critical Text and the Text underlying our King James Bible (Cf. **BFT #3084**). This, to me, is very disturbing.

STATEMENT #104: (p. 94) "*These <u>seven points</u> evaluate each reading by asking respectively: How ancient is the wording? How many manuscripts support the reading? How widespread is the support? . . .*"

COMMENT #104: The authors list Dean John W. Burgon's "*<u>seven tests of truth</u>.*" They are very good tests. A very important test is that of "*variety*" which means different kinds of evidence which have been spread out over many countries and from many centuries. That is what the Textus Receptus that underlies the King James Bible has.

Dean Burgon "Convinced" Many

STATEMENT #105: (p. 94) "*Although Burgon exercised admirable thoroughness in examining textual evidence, his refutation of Hort's procedures and conclusions <u>convinced few textual researchers</u>.*"

COMMENT #105: Dean Burgon has certainly "*<u>convinced</u>*" me of the defense of the Traditional Greek text. I read of Dean Burgon first in Dr. David Otis Fuller's book *Which Bible.* It was a condensed version of

Burgon's *Revision Revised.* I read Dean Burgon even though he was an Anglican of the Church of England and I am a Baptist. I read him and I loved his facts, his wording, his documentation, and his spirit.

Even though they say Dean Burgon "*convinced few textual researchers*," there has been a society in memory of Dean Burgon. I have been the President of the Dean Burgon Society since its founding in 1978. This is an active Society that meets each year with more than seventeen speakers "IN DEFENSE OF TRADITIONAL BIBLE TEXTS."

Its messages are transmitted all over the world on its Website, DeanBurgon Society.org. There are nineteen members of the DBS Executive Committee and as of this writing, fifteen more members of the DBS Advisory Council. These represent Pastors and laymen from the USA and the foreign countries of Canada, the United Kingdom, Australia, and Singapore. It truly is an international ministry and outreach. Its radio programs are aired in this country and by Shortwave around the world each week. A number of people are waking up to the truth through its ministry.

The DBS has reprinted five of Dean Burgon's books in hardback editions:

(1) *The Last Twelve Verses of Mark* (BFT #1139 @ $15 + $5 S&H);

(2) *The Revision Revised* (BFT #611 @ $25 + $5 S&H);

(3) *The Traditional Text* (BFT #1159 @ $15 + $5 S&H);

(4) *The Causes of Corruption of the Traditional Text*; (BFT #1160 @ $16 + $5 S&H), and

(5) *Inspiration and Interpretation* (BFT #1220 @ $25 + $5 S&H).

All of these can be ordered at the DBS Website (DeanBurgonSociety. org) and also at the BFT Website (BibleForToday.org).

STATEMENT #106: (p. 95) "*Thus, Burgon's influence continues, and his **books** remain in print through the efforts of some of his own modern heirs.*"

COMMENT #106: This is a true statement. There is a footnote #47, but there is no mention of the Dean Burgon Society (Box 354, or c/o 900 Park Avenue, Collingswood, New Jersey). It talks about Dean Burgon's **books**, but makes no mention that the Dean Burgon Society published all six of these major **books** on textual matters in hardback editions, or that they are available through either the DBS or the BIBLE FOR TODAY at 900 Park Avenue, Collingswood, New Jersey 08108 **(Phone: 856-854-4452).**

STATEMENT #107: (p. 95) Their conclusion stated: "*The goal of this chapter has been to present the historical background for **modern theories***

of textual criticism."

COMMENT #107: They certainly did not do a thorough job in presenting the views of Dean Burgon and his *"modern"* followers. For this, I would recommend all of the above-mentioned books by Dean Burgon and also a book by Dean Burgon's understudy, Rev. Edward Miller entitled *A Guide to Textual Criticism* by Edward Miller (BFT #743 @ $12 + $4 S&H). It has a much better analysis and is a much better work as far as defining what the textual criticism should be rather than the false methodology of Westcott and Hort.

"Doctrine" Is Affected

STATEMENT #108: (p. 96) *". . . Bengel proved that manuscript variation does not affect doctrine, and his theories earned him the title Father of Textual Criticism."*

COMMENT #108: Bengel's position on *"doctrine"* and these BJU writers should not agree with it. When are they going to get truthful and honest about this question of *"doctrine"* and *"manuscript variation"*? Once again I invite the reader to get a copy and study Dr. Jack Moorman's 100-page document on *356 Doctrinal Passages in the NIV and Its Underlying Greek Text* (BFT #2956 @ $10 + $4 S&H). In certain places: the doctrine of the Virgin Birth is denied. The doctrine of Christ is also denied. The doctrine of Christ's Deity is denied. The doctrine of miracles is denied. The doctrine that Christ is the Creator of all things is denied. You should stick to the King James Bible wherein in truth no *"doctrine"* is affected or denied.

STATEMENT #109: (p. 96) *"Erasmus buckled under the pressure of tradition regarding the Comma Johanneum [1 John 5:7-8]. Burgon also erred in adopting tradition as evidence of preservation."*

COMMENT #109: These men do not accept 1 John 5:7-8 as genuine. I accept it. Dr. Jack Moorman has an excellent fifteen-page summary of the evidence in support of these verses (Cf. BFT #2249 @ $2 + $1 S&H).

Burgon did not err in using *"tradition"* as *"evidence of preservation"* when the *"tradition"* took the form of either

(1) uncial manuscripts,

(2) cursive manuscripts,

(3) papyri manuscripts,

(4) the readings of early versions, or

(5) quotations from early church fathers. All five of these *"traditions"* are indeed evidentiary.

"Word" Preserved Not "Words"

STATEMENT #110:   (p. 97) *"Perhaps the most important conclusion drawn by all of these men is that the <u>Word of God</u> has been <u>preserved.</u>"*

   COMMENT #110: What do they mean by "<u>Word of God</u>"? Here again these authors are referring to God's "<u>Word</u>" instead of God's "<u>Words</u>." By this term they believe that God has preserved only His *"ideas, thoughts, concepts, message, truth, or teachings,"* rather than the original Hebrew, Aramaic, and Greek <u>Words</u>. In the Bible, the <u>Word</u> of God is equal to the <u>Words</u> of God.

When David wrote *"Thy <u>Word</u> have I hid in mine heart, that I might not sin against thee"* (Psalm 119:11), he was referring to the <u>Words</u> of God.

   It is deceptively not so with these Fundamentalist brethren writing this book *Bible Preservation and the Providence of God.* It is not so with the Bob Jones University-approved authors of the book, *God's <u>Word</u> in our Hands.* These books from the Bob Jones University frame of mind and background redefine "<u>WORD</u>." Here are Schnaiter and Tagliapietra, both staff members at Bob Jones University teaching these errors to their students who will go out into the highways and byways with the wrong doctrine about the Bible and its *"<u>preservation.</u>"* They have a false and heretical view of Bible *"<u>preservation.</u>"*

"Doctrines" Are "In Question"

STATEMENT #111: (p. 97) *". . . they disagree on the manner and details. All of them agree that <u>not a single doctrine of Scripture is in question.</u>"*

   COMMENT #111:   As I have said before, that is an absolutely false and misleading statement. Once again I invite the reader to get a copy and study Dr. Jack Moorman's 100-page document on *356 Doctrinal Passages in the NIV and Its Underlying Greek Text* **(BFT #2956 @ $10 + $4 S&H).** For them to say that *<u>not a single doctrine of Scripture is in question</u>* is grossly untrue and deceptive.

STATEMENT #112: (p. 98) [They are quoting from Dean Burgon] *"The provision, then, which the Divine Author of Scripture found to have been made for <u>the preservation in its integrity of His written Word</u>, is of a peculiarly varied and highly complex description. First,--by causing the vast multiplication of copies should be required all down the ages, . . . He provided the most effectual security imaginable against fraud. . . . Next, versions . . . lastly . . . patristic citations accordingly are a third mighty safeguard of the integrity of the deposit."*

COMMENT #112: This is a good quotation from Dean Burgon. Notice that he believed in "*the preservation in its integrity of His written Word*." By that he means the "**Words**," not just the "*ideas, thoughts, concepts, message, truth, or teachings*," as these authors believe.

STATEMENT #113: (p. 102) [In a question section, they asked to] "*List Westcott and Hort's three key arguments against the Syrian text type.*"

COMMENT #113: I do not accept "*text types*" as I have explained before. This is just another one of Westcott and Hort's lies against the Textus Receptus. The authors want the reader of their book to repeat the "*three key arguments*" against the Hebrew, Aramaic, and Greek **Words** underlying the King James Bible. Every one of these arguments is fallacious and untrue.

CHAPTER 6
GENERAL MODERN THEORIES

STATEMENT #114: (p. 103) [This is from Chapter Six, "General Modern Theories"] "*Second, there is a limited number of possible theories explaining textual variants. One view promotes a single conservative manuscript or version as the best, one adheres to a single text type as the best, and one selects readings from different manuscripts or text types on the basis of various theoretical criteria.*"

COMMENT #114: These three "*possible theories*" are all based on the wrong premise.

A chief cause of "*textual variants*" is the contamination made by early heretics to conform the Bible to their own false doctrines. This process operated to the greatest degree during the first hundred years after the New Testament was written.

The Vatican ("B") and Sinai ("Aleph") manuscripts are examples of this textual perversion. I take the New Testament **Words** to be accurate that have been given to us in the proper manuscripts, used in the proper early versions, and quoted or alluded to in the proper early church fathers. These are the **Words** that underlie our King James Bible.

"Orthodoxy" Is "Disturbed"

STATEMENT #115: (p. 103) "*Third, and most important, none of these views necessarily disturbs the orthodoxy of the Christian Church as plainly taught in the Scriptures.*"

COMMENT #115: The false Westcott and Hort view of the Bible does "*disturb*" and undermine the "*orthodoxy*" of the Christian Church. It undermines it because it takes away the Christian Church's "*Scriptures*." Once again I invite the reader to get a copy and study Dr. Jack Moorman's 100-large-page documentation on *356 Doctrinal Passages in the NIV and Its Underlying Greek Text* (BFT #2956 @ $10 + $4 S&H). This is an important subject to study and to answer to the satisfaction of all the members of our churches.

"Eclectic" Not "Eclectic"

STATEMENT #116: (p. 104) "*In textual criticism the term eclectic simply describes the process of selecting readings from various manuscripts and text types.*"

COMMENT #116: This is in fact what modern "*textual criticism*" does not do. They follow the Vatican ("B") and Sinai ("Aleph") manuscripts and the forty-three or so that follow them and leave the other more than 5,000 manuscripts alone. They say these are inferior and should not be followed under any circumstances. This is the height of deception, hypocrisy, and falsehood.

More Than A "Small Proportion"

STATEMENT #117: (p. 105) "*Recall that there is only a small proportion of passages where manuscripts substantially disagree.*"

COMMENT #117: This is false. As I have said before, in the New Testament, Dr. Jack Moorman has outlined over 8,000 differences between the Greek Text of Nestle/Aland and the Greek Text underlying the King James Bible. It is a result of hundreds of hours of research. It gives the Greek **Words** and the English translations. This book of over 500-large-pages on "*8,000 Differences between the NIV and Modern Versions and the Words Underlying the King James Bible*" is available from the BIBLE FOR TODAY for a gift of $65.00 + $7.50 S&H. It is BFT #3084. Though obviously some of these are small differences, but many are "*substantial.*" Once again I invite the reader to get a copy and study Dr. Jack Moorman's 100-page document on *356 Doctrinal Passages in the NIV and Its Underlying Greek Text* (BFT #2956 @ $10 + $4 S&H). These are "*substantial,*" and there are hundreds more among the 8,000 differences in the Greek **Words**.

STATEMENT #118: (p. 105) "*Metzger and Aland believe that such problems are best resolved by evaluating all available evidence, which includes date and place of manuscripts as well as author's style and scribal habits.*"

COMMENT #118: This again is a false statement. These Critical Text followers do not resolve "*problems*" by "*evaluating all available evidence.*" Instead, they see what the Vatican and Sinai manuscripts and their few followers have, and follow it.

> An example of this is how these people deal with Mark 16:9-20. They did not resolve this by "*evaluating all available evidence.*" They did not make use of all the manuscripts. If these textual critics had done so, they would have accepted Mark 16:9-20 as genuine because all of the available evidence is there.

In Dean Burgon's day, there were 118 uncial manuscripts that have these verses. About 600 cursive manuscripts have them. Every Lectionary in the East has them. If they would accept all of these manuscripts, they would accept Mark 16:9-20. In Dean Burgon's day, the only two manuscripts that eliminated these twelve verses were the Vatican ("B") and the Sinai ("Aleph"). Rather than "*evaluating all available evidence,*" it seems to me that they have been "*rejecting all available evidence.*"

STATEMENT #119: (p. 105) "*Such evidence is handled much as in a court of law. Legal matters in the Bible required **multiple independent witnesses**. The greater the number of witnesses the less likelihood of a wrong judgment.*"

COMMENT #119: That is what we have in our King James Bible, a greater number of "*independent witnesses,*" and therefore the less likelihood of wrong judgment. I would rather stick to the Old Testament and New Testament of our King James Bible any day rather than any of these new versions which, in the New Testament, are limited to the dwarfed number of manuscripts of the corrupted Vatican and Sinai and the few others that mimic them.

STATEMENT #120: (p. 105) "*The basic idea is that the reading with the most **independent witnesses** from the most time periods (including the oldest) and geographical regions is most likely authentic*"

COMMENT #120: These principles are exactly what Dean Burgon agreed with and practiced. This is what led him to the defense of the Traditional Text and to the King James Bible. These principles are what the Westcott and Hort followers refused to accept.

"Canons" Were Rigged

STATEMENT #121: (p. 107) "*Prefer the **shorter reading**. This rule is the most famous. . . . Researchers use this **canon** extensively.*"

COMMENT #121: This is one of the several "_canons of criticism_" which were invented by Westcott and Hort in order to prove that the Vatican ("B") manuscript was the best of all. They are all based on this root goal. Each "**canon**" points to the Vatican ("B"). They believed the harder to understand reading is better than the easier to understand reading. Vatican wins. They believed that the"_shorter reading_" is better than the longer reading. Vatican wins. They believed the one that harmonizes is better than the one that does not. Vatican wins. They believed that the reading with the poorest grammar is better than the one with the best grammar. Vatican wins. It is like someone making up the clues for a treasure hunt. Each clue points to the treasure.

> So with Westcott and Hort. Their "_canons_" or clues were made up by them to point to their "_treasure_," manuscripts Vatican and Sinai ("B" and "Aleph").

Every one of these so-called "_canons_" are in error and attempt to lead people away from the true **Words** that underlie the King James Bible.

"Probabilities" Not the Way to Go

STATEMENT #122: (p. 109) "_. . . both types of internal evidence are called probabilities. Yet within internal evidence, **transcriptional probability** is **less subjective** than **intrinsic probability**, since typical scribal copying errors are better known than the styles of the human authors themselves._"

COMMENT #122: They imply that "_intrinsic probability_" is more "_subjective_" than "_transcriptional probability_." In point of fact, neither of these "_probabilities_" thought up by Westcott and Hort are true. They are both subjective and not objective in any way. They are all guess work and hypothesis.

> The "_transcriptional probability_" is a pure guess as to what a scribe would write. How does anyone know what a scribe would write? "_Intrinsic probability_" means what would James, Paul, John, Peter or other writers of the Bible put down in their original writing. What is the "_probability_" that the writer would write this or that word?

These critics then change the Bible's **Words** on the basis of pure guesswork.

"Preserved" Only the "Word"

STATEMENT #123: (p. 111) "_. . . suggests a **weaker view of preservation** than Fundamentalists take. It shows that they do not consider the_ *mass of manuscript evidence to have **definitely preserved the Word of God** to the present."*

COMMENT #123: Here again these authors are referring to God's "**Word**" instead of God's "**Words**." By this term they believe that God has preserved only His "*ideas, thoughts, concepts, message, truth, or teachings,*" rather than the original Hebrew, Aramaic, and Greek **Words**. It seems that they are doubting that God has "***definitely preserved***" His **Words**.

> The Lord Jesus Christ said: *"Heaven and earth shall pass away, but my **Words** shall not pass away"* (Matthew 24:35; Mark 13:31; Luke 21:33). We have every right to believe that God has not only promised to preserve His **Words**, but that He has fulfilled that promise.

This is what we hold to in our BIBLE FOR TODAY and our Dean Burgon Society.

STATEMENT #124: (p. 112) *"Second, their popular books have served to stabilize terminology in the field. The bewildering maze of names, for the **text types** . . ."*

COMMENT #124: They are talking about these most recent writers who have written many books on textual criticism. They think this is all right. I would disagree, because with few exceptions, the modern books are written from the false Westcott and Hort side of the issue.

KJV & Traditional Text Not Erasmus

STATEMENT #125: (p. 115) [This section is on the Textus Receptus] *"This included the Byzantine Manuscripts, the Textus Receptus of Erasmus. **In English the KJV is the Traditional Text, which is based on Erasmus**."*

COMMENT #125: This sentence assumes two things, both of which are false.

(1) In the first place, the "***Traditional Text***" was not "***based on Erasmus***." It was the other way around. Erasmus took the traditional manuscripts and put them into printed form. This is implied throughout this book and others written by the Bob Jones University groups.

(2) In the second place, this sentence also implies that the "**KJV . . . was based on Erasmus**." His first edition was made in 1516. His Greek text was not the basis of the King James Bible. It was rather that of Beza's 5th edition of 1598, eighty-two years later. The Bob Jones University group continues to repeat this lie over and over again. When will they stop lying about the basis of the King James Bible? Cannot we agree on anything? Cannot these Fundamentalists from Bob Jones University, Central Baptist Seminary, Detroit Baptist Seminary, Calvary Baptist Seminary, and other schools in this orbit

agree on this?

Erasmus (1516) was not the originator of the Textus Receptus and Erasmus (1516) was not the basis of the King James Bible.

TR Not From "Handful" of MSS

STATEMENT #126: (p. 115) *"The Textus Receptus (TR), which came from a handful of manuscripts of the Byzantine type, includes a peculiarity here and there not typical of the entire Byzantine family or text type."*

COMMENT #126: This lie is repeated once again. They say that "*Textus Receptus (TR), . . . came from a handful of manuscripts*." They say it came from Erasmus whom they say had only a "*handful of manuscripts*." The Textus Receptus or Traditional Text does not just have a "*handful of manuscripts*."

As a matter of fact, the Textus Receptus or Traditional Text is based on over 99% of the manuscripts that have been preserved up to now.

In Kurt Aland's day of 1967 (he is dead now), he said there were 5,255 Greek manuscripts. Dr. Jack Moorman has analyzed those manuscripts and has put some in the Textus Receptus type and others in the Westcott and Hort (or the "B" and "Aleph") type of manuscripts. He has found that "B" and "Aleph" and about forty-three other Greek manuscripts (less than 1%) go along with the modern text of Westcott and Hort. The rest of them, 5,210 Greek manuscripts (over 99%), go along with the Textus Receptus or the Received Text, which underlies our King James Bible. That is much more than a "*handful.*"

"Message Pure" Only, not "Words"

STATEMENT #127: (p. 118) [talking about Dr. Edward Hills] *"However, to claim that only one view is Biblical, it is necessary to show that no other view is compatible with Scripture. Has Hills proved this? Certainly not. The Scriptures he cited prove only that God has kept His message pure to the present and do not say anything about how God has preserved it."*

COMMENT #127: Here again these men are saying that God has only "kept His Message pure to the present," but they do not say or believe, as I do, that He has kept His Hebrew, Aramaic, and Greek **Words**. You can have a "*message*," but if you do not have the exact **Words** of that "*message*," you are at a loss. You must know exactly what is being communicated. We must communicate in **words** to maintain clarity. In the Bible, God communicated in Hebrew, Aramaic, and Greek **Words**. He wants us to study those **Words** to be completely clear on what He means.

STATEMENT #128: (p. 118) "... (*Matthew 24:35*) "*Heaven and earth shall pass away, but my <u>Words</u> shall not pass away" does not identify any manuscript or text type or whether the preservation will be achieved through popular texts, traditional texts, old texts, or simply some text somewhere on earth or in heaven. <u>These authoritative words of Jesus guarantee only that his Word will be preserved</u>* and that none of His <u>words</u> will be lost."

COMMENT #128: Though they use "<u>words</u>," they say only his "<u>Word will be preserved</u>." Here again these authors are referring to God's "<u>Word</u>" instead of God's "<u>Words</u>." By this term they believe that God has preserved only His "*ideas, thoughts, concepts, message, truth, or teachings,*" rather than the original Hebrew, Aramaic, and Greek <u>Words</u>. These Bob Jones University men have a big question mark about what <u>Words</u> are going to pass away and the method of keeping them so they will not "*<u>pass away</u>*."

> I believe the Lord Jesus Christ is the Author of all the Hebrew, Aramaic, and Greek <u>Words</u> of the Old and the New Testaments. He is the Teacher Who communicated to God the Holy Spirit all of the <u>Words</u> to give to the human writers (John 16:12-14).

"God Preserved" Only "His Word"

STATEMENT #129: (p. 119) "*What is at issue is not whether <u>God preserved His Word</u>, but how God superintended the preservation of His <u>Word</u>.*"

COMMENT #129:

> Here again these authors are referring to God's "<u>Word</u>" instead of God's "<u>Words</u>." By this term they believe that God has "*<u>preserved</u>*" only His "*ideas, thoughts, concepts, message, truth, or teachings,*" rather than the original Hebrew, Aramaic, and Greek <u>Words</u>.

STATEMENT #130: (p. 119) "*Third, the real Satanic attacks on the <u>Word</u> of God during the manuscript period took the same form that they now take today: <u>denying, misinterpreting, mistranslating, and misapplying</u> the <u>Word</u>.*"

COMMENT #130: Let me repeat it once again. By using "<u>Word</u>," they believe that God has preserved only His "*ideas, thoughts, concepts, message, truth, or teachings,*" rather than the original Hebrew, Aramaic, and Greek <u>Words</u>. By this technique, these authors are "*<u>denying, misinterpreting , . . and misapplying</u>*" God's <u>Words</u>.

Doctrine Is Affected

STATEMENT #131:   (p. 120)   *"The <u>variants</u> have minimal importance to <u>preservation</u> because they are comparatively <u>few</u>, and because <u>no Christian doctrine is affected</u> by them."*

COMMENT #131: They are wrong in two areas by this sentence.   (1) The *"<u>variants</u>"* are not *"<u>comparatively few</u>."*   As I have mentioned before, Dr. Jack Moorman's 500-large-page research has catalogued **over 8,000 differences** between the Critical Text and the Text underlying our King James Bible (Cf. **BFT #3084** @ **$65.00 + $7.50 S&H**). 8,000 *"<u>variants</u>"* are not a *"<u>few</u>."* (2) *"Christian doctrine"* <u>is</u> *"affected."* Once again I invite the reader to get a copy and study Dr. Jack Moorman's 100-page document on *356 Doctrinal Passages in the NIV and Its Underlying Greek Text* (**BFT #2956** @ **$10 + $4 S&H**). There are 356 *"doctrinal passages"* affected by the false text of "B" and "Aleph" and these new translations.

"Doctrine Is Lost"

STATEMENT #132: (p. 122) *"<u>No doctrine is lost</u>, all the <u>Words</u> are <u>preserved in the mass of manuscript evidence</u>. . . ."*

COMMENT #132:   As I mentioned above, I invite the reader to get a copy and study Dr. Jack Moorman's 100-page document on *356 Doctrinal Passages in the NIV and Its Underlying Greek Text* (**BFT #2956** @ **$10 + $4 S&H**). The doctrines that are involved are not present in the manuscripts of these authors from Bob Jones University, namely those of Westcott and Hort, of Nestle-Aland, or of United Bible Societies. These editions do not have 356 doctrinal passages correct. They are incorrect. For this book to say that *"<u>no doctrine is lost</u>"* is absolutely false and deceptive indeed. If you have the Textus Receptus, nothing is lost in doctrine, but if you are following the doctrine and teachings of the false Greek text that is used at Bob Jones University, you have 356 doctrines which are questioned.

CHAPTER 7

REFINEMENTS

STATEMENT #133: (p. 134) [This is Chapter Seven, "Refinements" under the caption "The Majority Text"] *"As evidence, he sights* [that is Pickering] *some intemperate statements of Hort who referred to the Textus Receptus as 'vile' and 'corrupt' and the like. <u>He thus portrays Hort's theory as unobjective, biased, and therefore untrustworthy</u>."*

COMMENT #133: It is true that *"Hort's theory [is] unobjective, biased, and therefore untrustworthy."* These authors do not agree with this. They defend Westcott and Hort's false Greek Text and the theory that underlies it. Westcott and Hort had an axe to grind.

> **Their main purpose was to change, uproot, and dethrone our King James Bible and the Words that underlie it.**

STATEMENT #134: (pp. 135-36) *"However, the key weakness of the Majority Text position is not any weak arguments against eclecticism, but rather the lack of ancient manuscripts supporting it. If its proponents would hold up an ancient manuscript as a proof of its antiquity, its detractors would be silenced."*

COMMENT #134: I defend the Textus Receptus, not the so-called *"Majority Text"* which changes the TR in over 1,800 places. *"Ancient manuscripts"* are just one part of *"antiquity."*

> **The most important part of *"antiquity"* are the *"ancient"* Words, not the age of the material on which these Words are written. Proof of these *"ancient"* Words is found in the early versions or translations and in the quotations or allusions found in the early church fathers. The Words of the Textus Receptus have *"antiquity"* by comparisons of early versions and in the early church father's quotations.**

The evidences for the last twelve verses of Mark (Mark 16:9-20) show its *"antiquity."* Numbers of manuscripts are very important. In Dean Burgon's day, not only were there 118 uncial manuscripts, about 600 cursive manuscripts, and every Lectionary in the East that had these verses; but also ten of the ancient versions that had them. Many of these versions are more *"ancient"* than either the Vatican or Sinai manuscripts which omit the verses. There are also nineteen of the ancient church fathers who quoted from these verses. Many of these fathers are more *"ancient"* than either the Vatican or Sinai manuscripts.

STATEMENT #135: (p. 136) *"Some who hold to the Eclectic view are far quicker to publicly defend the inspiration, inerrancy and preservation of the Bible than were Metzger and Aland."*

COMMENT #135: Some of these are teachers at Bob Jones University. They may defend *"inspiration"* and *"inerrancy,"* but they believe the Bible is *"preserved"* in the false text of Nestle-Aland or that of the United Bible Societies rather than in the Textus Receptus underlying the King James Bible. They also, like these authors, deny the preservation of the Words of the

Bible, but only the <u>Word</u>, by which they mean only the *"ideas, thoughts, concepts, message, truth, or teachings"* of the Bible, but not the <u>Words</u>.

False "Preservation" Of "Scriptures"

STATEMENT #136: (p. 136) *"First, conservative Eclecticism takes a <u>clear stand</u> for divine inspiration and <u>preservation of the Scriptures</u>."*

COMMENT #136: They take a false view of the *"<u>preservation of the Scriptures</u>."* Theirs is not a *"<u>clear stand</u>"* at all. It is a deceptive *"<u>stand</u>."* They do not believe that the <u>Words</u> of the Bible were preserved. Schnaiter, Tagliapietra, and the entire Bob Jones University faculty in general take this false position. It is the same position taken by the Bob Jones University-backed books, *From the Mind of God to the Mind of Man* and *God's <u>Word</u> in our Hands.* The first book I have answered in *Fundamentalist Mis-Information on Bible Versions* (BFT #2974 @ $7.00 + $3 S&H). The second book I have answered in *Fundamentalist Deception on Bible Preservation* (BFT #3234 @ $8.00 + $3 S&H). They believe only in the preservation of the <u>Word</u> of God, by which they mean *"ideas, thoughts, concepts, message, truth, or teachings,"* but not the Hebrew, Aramaic, and Greek <u>Words</u> of the originals. Their preservation is extremely partial.

STATEMENT #137: (pp. 136-37) *"Similarly D. A. Carson defends both inspiration and inerrancy. . . . The Scripture is <u>preserved in the mass</u> of manuscript evidence."*

COMMENT #137: D. A. Carson is one of the most foremost opponents of the Textus Receptus. He certainly does not believe in Bible preservation of the <u>Words</u> of Scripture because he has different preservation than we have in our Textus Receptus. If the Bible is only *"<u>preserved in the mass of manuscript evidence</u>,"* that is no *"<u>preservation</u>."* *"<u>Preservation</u>"* of something means that you can find it. It is not a needle in a haystack that takes hundreds or hours of searching.

STATEMENT #138: (p. 137) *"The agreement of the mass of manuscripts is the key problem confronting <u>eclectic scholars</u>."*

COMMENT #138: This is something that should affect them. There is an agreement in about 99% of the 5,255 manuscripts catalogued by Kurt Aland as of 1967. The manuscripts, which are closest in agreement, are the Traditional Textus Receptus Greek Manuscripts, not the manuscripts that they hold to of the Critical Text. The Critical Text has less than 1% of these manuscripts. It takes a great amount of falsehood and fictitious stories for these so-called *"<u>eclectic scholars</u>"* to explain this truth away.

STATEMENT #139: (p. 139) *"Instead, its claim for authenticity depends on a <u>handful of manuscripts</u>, though very ancient ones. The lack, then,* *of a large quantity of manuscripts with the disputed readings is the primary problem with which the theory must wrestle."*

COMMENT #139: This is an important admission on the part of these two Westcott and Hort followers. They admit that this false Critical Text depends on just a "*handful of manuscripts*." This is true. Dr. Jack Moorman, in his book *Forever Settled* (BFT #1428 @ $20.00 + $5 S&P) has analyzed the manuscripts that favor the Westcott and Hort Greek Critical Text. He comes up with the Vatican ("B") and the Sinai ("Aleph") manuscripts and forty-three others that agree with them, making a total of only forty-five manuscripts of the false variety that have survived the ages. This is less than 1% of the 5,255 manuscripts catalogued by Kurt Aland in 1967. The remainder, or 5,210 Greek manuscripts, or over 99% of the evidence, comes down on the side of the Traditional Textus Receptus that underlies our King James Bible. That is a very important and revealing admission.

STATEMENT #140: (p. 143) [This is in the conclusion of this chapter] "*The three positions presented in this chapter build on the positions previously presented. The **Majority Text** view of **Pickering and Hodges** build a stronger case even than the Textus Receptus view of Burgon and Hills while still retaining its strengths.*"

COMMENT #140: The "*Textus Receptus view of Burgon and Hills*" is a much stronger position than the tentative and weak position of "*Pickering and Hodges*." I disagree with their assessment completely. For an excellent critique of the failures of the so-called "*Majority Text*" of Hodges and Farstad the reader should get *Hodges/Farstad's Majority Text Refuted* by Dr. Jack Moorman (BFT #1617 @ $16.00 + $5 S&H). After studying this document, the reader will have no confidence in this "*Majority Text*" but will cling even more strongly to the Textus Receptus underlying the King James Bible. For a thorough documentation on the superiority of the Traditional Textus Receptus, you should get four of Dean John W. Burgon's books: (1) *The Last Twelve Verses of Mark* (BFT #1139 @ $15.00 + $4 S&H); (2) *The Revision Revised* (BFT #611 @ $25.00 + $5 S&H); (3) *The Traditional Text of the Gospels* (BFT #1159 @ $15.00 + $5 S&H); and (4) *The Causes of the Corruption of the Traditional Text* (BFT #1160 @ $16.00 + $5.S&H).

CHAPTER 8
EXTREME VIEWS
No "Text Types"

STATEMENT #141: (p. 148) [From Chapter Eight, "Extreme Views" beginning with "*radical eclecticism*"] "*First, they reject the **text types**. They* argue that since the history of each manuscript is untraceable, the groupings into types are artificial, <u>**superficial and ultimately meaningless**</u>."

COMMENT #141: That is my view exactly and that of Dean John William Burgon. It is "<u>*superficial and ultimately meaningless*</u>" to have "<u>*text types*</u>."

STATEMENT #142: (p. 148) *"The rejection of <u>text types</u> by radical eclecticism (first distinctive) is logically neither a strength or weakness. However, it does serve a strengthening role within eclecticism since it reminds those who use text types that it is <u>a theory</u> and to <u>use it with caution</u>."*

COMMENT #142: I agree that it is "<u>*a theory*</u>," but I disagree that we should "<u>*use it with caution*</u>." Do not use it at all. There is no proof whatsoever for this, therefore it should not be any part of the New Testament textual consideration. Do you know who made this "<u>*theory*</u>" acceptable? It was none other than the heretics Westcott and Hort in their *Introduction* to their false Greek text that came out in 1881.

It Is "Guessing" For Them

STATEMENT #143: (p. 151) *"As we have shown in Chapters 2-4, God has <u>preserved His Word</u>, and <u>there is no need for guessing what He said in numerous passages</u>."*

COMMENT #143: Here again these authors are referring to God's "<u>**Word**</u>" instead of God's "<u>**Words**</u>." By this term they believe that God has preserved only His "*ideas, thoughts, concepts, message, truth, or teachings*" rather than the original Hebrew, Aramaic, and Greek <u>**Words**</u>. This is no "*preservation*" at all. We do not need to have "<u>*guessing*</u>" for any of God's preserved original Hebrew, Aramaic, and Greek <u>**Words**</u>.

STATEMENT #144: (p. 152) *"However, both points defy orthodox Christian views of <u>preservation</u>."*

COMMENT #144: Then they go on to talk about the "<u>*preservation*</u>" of God's <u>**Word**</u>, meaning only the "*ideas, thoughts, concepts, message, truth, or teachings*" of the Bible, but not the original Hebrew, Aramaic, and Greek <u>**Words**</u>. They talk about providential preservation of Scripture, but they do not mean the <u>**Words**</u> of God, only the meaning. This is the deception of these authors.

"B" & "Aleph" Not "Close" to "Perfect"

STATEMENT #145: (p. 154) [They are talking about the "King James Only" as a point of view] *"Of the many possible manuscripts and versions, few have ever been promoted as perfect. We have already seen that <u>no manuscript has ever been promoted as perfect</u> (though <u>Sinaiticus and</u>*

Vaticanus came as close as any.)"

    COMMENT #145: This is the most ridiculous statement made thus far. Far from *"Sinaiticus and Vaticanus"* being *"perfect,"* they are out of line in over 8,000 places with the **Words** underlying our King James Bible. These writers are in serious error on this point. They are also in serious error when they wrote that *"no manuscript has ever been promoted as perfect."* Are they so out of touch with reality that they have never heard of the verbal plenary preservation (VPP) of the Hebrew, Aramaic, and Greek **Words** that underlie the King James Bible. There is a growing group of us who believe this. It is time for the Bob Jones University crowd to recognize it. These people are all around the world, in Australia, in England, in Singapore, in Canada, in the United States, and in other places as well. There are men in churches, in radio ministries, in the classrooms, in theological seminaries, in Christian colleges, in written ministries, and on the mission fields, both at home and abroad, who stand with us in this Biblical doctrine of verbal plenary preservation of the Hebrew, Aramaic, and Greek **Words** of the Bible.

    Far from being *"perfect"* or even coming "as close as any," the Vatican and Sinai manuscripts have 8,000 differences between the Textus Receptus and them. How can they be close to *"perfect"*? They are the most imperfect manuscripts on the face of the earth as Dean Burgon has shown in his four books listed above.

> The Vatican ("B") and the Sinai ("Aleph") manuscripts have important differences between themselves in over 3,000 places in the Gospels alone! They have 356 doctrines, which are incorrect. They have left out 2,886 Greek **Words** that are in the King James Bible's text.

KJV Not "God's Inspired Word"

    STATEMENT #146: (p. 155) *"The KJV Only position, then, goes beyond preference and stands outside theories of manuscript evidence. Most KJV only advocates believe that the **King James Version** is the only English translation that could be called **God's inspired Word**. This means it is important that **inspiration** and preservation views surrounding it must exceed the **inspiration** which can be accorded to any other honest translations of the **Word** of God."*

    COMMENT #146:

> These writers are saying here that they believe translations can partake of *"inspiration."* This belief is rank heresy and Ruckmanism of the worst sort. I do not ever call the King James Bible *"inspired,"* *"inspired of God,"* *"God-breathed,"* or *"given by inspiration of God."*

The Greek word underlying those five words in 2 Timothy 3:16 is **THEOPNEUSTOS**. This comes from **THEOS** (God) and **PNEUSTOS** which comes from **PNEO** (to breathe). It means literally *"God breathed."* God did not breathe out English words. He breathed out Hebrew, Aramaic, and Greek **Words**. Those God-breathed **Words** are *"inspired by God."* That is the only *"inspiration"* there is. It was a once-for-all action by the Lord when making up the sixty-six books of the Bible. I do not say that the King James Bible is *"inspired."* What I do say about the King James Bible is this: **"Because of its accurate translation from the proper and preserved Hebrew, Aramaic, and Greek Words, the King James Bible, and only the King James Bible, can rightfully be called 'the Words of God in English.'"** This cannot honestly be said concerning any other English translation.

"Attacks" Doctrinal, Not "Personal"

STATEMENT #147: (p. 155) [They are talking about the people that are attacking the Westcott and Hort Text] *"Today, the leading advocate of this view is D. A. Waite, who has written an entire volume attacking Westcott and Hort personally."*

COMMENT #147: I have not *"attacked Westcott and Hort personally."* I have attacked their theology. I have attacked their beliefs. That is not a personal attack. They have a footnote on this noting the book I have written called, *"The Theological Heresies of Westcott and Hort."* This is **BFT #595 @ $7.00 + $2 S&H.** I took up their theological heresies one at a time. Since when is a difference in theology a personal attack? It is an attack on the theology of the men. Do you know what is in that book? I take five of their books, three from Westcott and two from Hort. I looked over every page of those five books. I took, in their own words, about 125 quotations from these books. The books I quoted from Westcott are: *The Gospel of John, The Epistles of John,* and *The Book of Hebrews.* The books I quoted from Hort are *1 Peter,* and *Revelation.*

> From these five books, I used 125 direct quotations, citing the pages in question. I have shown their theological heresies, without making a single statement questioning their honesty, their morals, or their character, or any other thing that honestly could be called a *"personal attack."*

If these two Bob Jones University staff men or any of their other staff can find such things, I would be glad to see them. They did not cite a single one of them because they could not find any.

STATEMENT #148: (p. 156) *"Some scholars dismiss all these writers as reactionaries or propagandists."*

COMMENT #148: Is this what these writers think I am? Since 1970 I have given studious years to the study, writing about, and defending the King James Bible and its underlying Hebrew, Aramaic, and Greek **Words**. These are important materials. I was attempting to upset and overthrow the false theories of Westcott and Hort, as well as the false theories of men like Schnaiter and Tagliapietra and educational institutions like Bob Jones University, whose views they represent.

"W & H" "Text" Was "Doctored"

STATEMENT #149: (p. 156) *"Donald A. Waite blatantly accuses Westcott and Hort of being, 'the prime movers in the elaborate-yet fictitious-system of New Testament Textual Criticism and the inventors of a doctored Greek text.'"*

COMMENT #149: Without the term *"blatantly,"* this is a correct quotation. There is also an endnote referencing *The Heresies of Westcott and Hort.* Westcott and Hort were *"prime movers"* and *"inventors of a doctored Greek text."* The readers can see exactly how it was *"doctored"* by getting a copy of D. A. Waite, Jr.'s excellent book, *The Doctored New Testament* (BFT #3138 @ $25+$5 S&H).

STATEMENT #150: (p. 157) *"A few KJV Only writers go considerably further. Some assert that no one is saved unless led to Christ using a King James Bible, or that foreign versions are not the Word of God unless translated from the KJV rather than Greek manuscripts."*

COMMENT #150: This is not my position, but that of Peter Ruckman and his followers. This is why I refuse to accept the term *"KJV Only,"* because it includes the Ruckmanites who do not in any way represent me.

STATEMENT #151: (p. 158) *" In other words, he [Peter Ruckman] viewed the translation as getting direct revelation from God concerning the correct translation, which offers such a degree of accuracy that the KJV can resolve textual issues among the Greek manuscripts."*

COMMENT #151: Again, I repeat, I do not want to be a part of *"KJV Onlyism"* because of the Ruckmanite inclusion. It is a smear term which does not include me. Ruckman's view that the Hebrew, Aramaic, and Greek can be *"corrected"* by the King James Bible is an outright heresy which I have exposed repeatedly ever since 1970.

STATEMENT #152: (p. 158) *"First of all, KJV Only advocates have by their very insistence on the preeminence on the King James Version, thereby emphasized that translations of the Word of God are in fact no less than the Word of God."*

COMMENT #152: Here again these authors are referring to God's "<u>Word</u>" instead of God's "<u>Words</u>." By this term, they believe that God has preserved only His "*ideas, thoughts, concepts, message, truth, or teachings*," rather than the original Hebrew, Aramaic, and Greek <u>Words</u>. Notice that they wrote about "*<u>translations</u>*" as if any translation for them would qualify as the "<u>Word</u> of God." Since they mean by the term "<u>Word</u>," only the "*ideas, thoughts, concepts, message, truth, or teachings*," for them it might be possible to term many "*<u>translations</u>*" as the "*<u>Word</u> of God*."

> "<u>Because of its accurate translation from the proper and preserved</u> <u>Hebrew, Aramaic, and Greek Words, the King James Bible, and only the</u> <u>King James Bible, can rightfully be called 'the Words of God in English.'"</u>

Be Cautious of Schools

STATEMENT #153: (p. 158) *"Second, the KJV Only position has attracted a large following due to its simplicity. Many Fundamentalists, especially those lacking training in Bible colleges or Christian universities or seminaries, would rather avoid troubling contentions about their 'final authority,' the Bible. <u>They naturally prefer to leave these matters to pastors and seminary professors</u>."*

COMMENT #153: Any who leave the matter of what the Bible is to seminary professors or staff workers, such as Samuel Schnaiter or Ron Tagliapietra, or to Bob Jones University who pays their salary (or to any other individuals or schools that agree with their position), will be in serious trouble with the true position of the Bible. True and faithful Bibliology (the doctrine of the Bible) has been, is now, and will be in the future completely torn to shreds by such people and the schools that employ them. Men who are training for the ministry should avoid such schools as Bob Jones University and the schools that back their false position. Do not send any such men to Detroit Baptist Seminary, to Central Baptist Seminary, to Calvary Baptist Seminary, to Northland Baptist Bible College, to Maranatha Baptist Bible College, or to any such Fundamentalist schools. They are false in what they believe on Bible texts, translations, and preservation. No, we should not look to such Christian universities and seminaries to tell us what to believe about the Bible.

Textual/Translational "Controversy"

STATEMENT #154: (p. 167) [From footnote #17] *"When we add to this the fact that some focus their ministry on <u>stirring up textual and translation controversy among Fundamentalists</u>, it is not surprising that we have such a tragic <u>schism</u> over these issues."*

COMMENT #154: The "_schism_" began when these writers and Bob Jones University openly departed from the preserved Hebrew, Aramaic, and Greek **Words** that underlie it. That is the source of the "_schism_." The present book that I am reviewing is doing exactly like it is accusing others of doing--causing a "_schism_" on the Bible. Do not blame the "_schism_" on those of us who are standing where we always stood on the King James Bible and its underlying **Words**. Yes, there is "_schism_." Yes, there is a controversy on the Bible among Fundamentalists. Why not bring it up? Why should our side keep silent when bold attacks against our position are being propounded in words and in print?

KJV Not From "Erasmus"

STATEMENT #155: (p. 159) _"To frivolously condemn scholarship condemns also **Erasmus**, the scholar who provided the Greek New Testament for the scholar Martin Luther to translate and the scholars of the King James Version **to translate into our KJV Bible**."_

COMMENT #155: The Greek text of "_Erasmus_" (1516 A.D.) was not the text on which the "_KJV Bible_" was based. It was that of Beza, 5th edition (1598 A.D) eighty-two years later. This lie and falsehood has been repeated by every approved book by Bob Jones University that comes off the presses. This book is no exception. When are they going to stop making this factual error?

STATEMENT #156: (p. 160) _"There are many godly men among **textual scholars** who help to warn God's people of errors from the **ungodly ones**."_

COMMENT #156: What does that mean? Do these two writers deny that I am a "_textual scholar_"? Do they think they and their false views on Bibliology are the only "_textual scholars_"? Or do they consider me to be "_ungodly_"? Or both? Is this because I think their positions on the Bible texts, translations, and preservation are in serious error? I certainly have more combined linguistic training in the Hebrew and Greek languages than either of these two authors, or any other professor at either Bob Jones University, Detroit Baptist Seminary, Central Baptist Seminary, Calvary Baptist Seminary, Northland Baptist Bible College, Maranatha Baptist Bible College or any of the other sister schools that follow these same errors.

If any of the teachers in any of these schools think they have earned more semester hours in these languages, (and have received better grades than I have), I strongly urge them to send me their transcripts to prove it, and I shall show them my own transcripts to prove them wrong. Here is a summary of my own linguistic training.

Lest some readers question my statements in this regard, let me quote from my book *The Case for the King James Bible* (BFT #83 @ $7.00+$3.00 S&H) concerning my satisfactory completion of various semester hours in either formal resident University or theological seminary training in the original Biblical and other foreign languages.

"*The writer was thoroughly prepared and trained in the original biblical languages of Hebrew and Greek. He received credit in these languages either at the University of Michigan (1945-48) or at the Dallas Theological Seminary (1948-53) as follows: In Greek, 66 semester hours; in Hebrew, 25 semester hours; a total of 91 semester hours in combined biblical languages.*

In addition to these 91 semester hours, the author has received credit for 27 additional hours in other foreign languages, divided as follows: Latin, 8 semester hours; French, 8 semester hours; Spanish, 11 semester hours. The grand total of foreign languages in terms of semester hours, in addition to the many other related courses taken at schools for work on the author's A.B., M.A., Th.M., Th.D., and/or Ph.D., has been 118 semester hours in foreign languages. This is only 2 semester hours short of a solid 4-year undergraduate course consisting of 120 semester hours required for graduation in most universities today.

Four of the five-residency-earned degrees mentioned above (M.A., Th.M., Th.D., and Ph.D.) required research theses and/or dissertations which prepared him to deal satisfactorily with documentation and evidence. Whatever other differences the modern critics of the King James Bible and its underlying Hebrew and Greek texts might have with this writer, they cannot justifiably criticize his preparations and training in these essential disciplines." [The Case for the King James Bible, p. 2]

Westcott & Hort Are The "Source"

STATEMENT #157: (p. 160) "*First the KJV Only position misapplies the logic of faith idea to polarize versions and manuscripts into those from God and those from the Devil. Westcott and Hort are vilified as the source of all modern theories and versions.*"

COMMENT #157: There is a polarization in the Bible texts, translations, and preservation arguments. These writers and Bob Jones University who employs them polarize themselves in favor of the Westcott and Hort Critical Text and they strongly oppose the **Words** that underlie the King James Bible. They are polarizing themselves against the King James Bible as to its veracity and underlying Hebrew, Aramaic, and Greek **Words**. On the other hand, they make room for other modern versions such as: The New

American Standard Version, the New King James Version, or the English Standard Version. Some Critical Text worshipers go even further and sanction the Revised Standard Version, the New Revised Standard Version, the New International Version, or other even farther out paraphrases.

It is false to say that I "*vilify Westcott and Hort*." "*Vilify*" is a term that means:

> "*to use abusive or slanderous language about or of;* calumniate; revile; defame."

I have never used "*slanderous language*" concerning these two men. I have proved my charges against their theology by using their own words. I would never term them heretics and apostates without their own words to prove my case. As I have mentioned before, these quotations are given in full in my book, *The Theological Heresies of Westcott and Hort.* This is BFT #595 @ $7.00 + $2 S&H.

Further quotations are found in my book, *Westcott's Clever Denial of Christ's Bodily Resurrection* (BFT #1131 @ $4.00 + $2 S&H). By their *Introduction* to their false Greek text of 1881, Westcott and Hort did lay the rational (though irrational) foundation that could be considered the "*source of all modern theories and versions*." This book itself admits that most of the present New Testament Greek editions are the same or similar to the edition of Westcott and Hort's in 1881.

STATEMENT #158: (p. 160) [They are talking about J. J. Ray] "*The premise enables him to evaluate other versions by comparing them side by side with the KJV and merely listing differences. Yet such writers denounce Hort for judging the TR as corrupt as compared with Vaticanus.*"

COMMENT #158: Hort should be "*denounced*" for "*judging the TR as corrupt as compared with Vaticanus*." The Vaticanus ("B") manuscript is seriously corrupt. The Textus Receptus manuscripts are the correct ones.

"Doubts" on "Doctrine"

STATEMENT #159: (p. 160) "*Mauro acknowledges that 'the sum of all the variant readings taken together does not give ground to the slightest doubt as to any of the fundamental points of faith and doctrine.*'"

COMMENT #159: That is a blatant falsehood. Once again I invite the reader to get a copy and study Dr. Jack Moorman's 100-page documentation on *356 Doctrinal Passages in the NIV and Its Underlying Greek Text* (BFT #2956 @ $10 + $4 S&H). Many of these 356 passages shed doubt on "*fundamental points of faith and doctrine*." These staff members from Bob Jones University should get this straight and cease lying to their readers, listeners, pastors, and students about this subject. To say falsely that doctrine is not involved, when doctrine is involved, does incalculable harm to those who are reading this Bob Jones University book. This is one solid reason why I am so strongly against this misleading and lying book.

KJV Not an "Inspired Translation"

STATEMENT #160: (p. 161) *"The final objections apply only to the most extreme branch of KJV Onlyism. Those who argue that in 1611 God guided the KJV translators to produce an __inspired translation__, trod theologically dangerous ground."*

COMMENT #160: Let me repeat what I say about the King James Bible: I do not ever call the King James Bible *"inspired," "inspired of God," "God-breathed,"* or *"given by inspiration of God."* The Greek word underlying those five words in 2 Timothy 3:16 is **THEOPNEUSTOS**. This comes from **THEOS** (God) and **PNEUSTOS** which comes from **PNEO** (to breathe). It means literally *"God breathed."*

God did not breathe out English words. He breathed out Hebrew, Aramaic, and Greek __Words__. Those God-breathed __Words__ are *"inspired by God."* That is the only *"inspiration"* there is. It was a once-for-all action by the Lord when making up the sixty-six books of the Bible. I do not say that the King James Bible is *"inspired."*

What I do say about the King James Bible is this: **"Because of its accurate translation from the proper and preserved Hebrew, Aramaic, and Greek Words, the King James Bible, and only the King James Bible, can rightfully be called 'the Words of God in English.'"** This cannot honestly be said concerning any other English translation.

Translations are not *"given by inspiration of God."* They are not *"God-breathed."* It does not matter if these translations are French, Spanish, Italian, Russian, or Chinese. Translations are not *"__inspired__."* I have never taught this. I believe we have to be very careful about this.

Our Dean Burgon Society, which I have led as President since 1978, has taken a position against the inspiration of the King James Bible or any other translation. We do not permit this teaching at any of our annual conferences. We feel it is part of the terminology of Ruckmanism and is in error, as well as being very confusing with the true and Biblical doctrine of the Divine inspiration of the Hebrew, Aramaic, and Greek __Words__ of the Bible.

STATEMENT #161: (p. 162) *"The accusation, then, misrepresents critical and __conservative eclectic scholars__ by __lumping__ them with the __radical__* *eclectic scholars.*"

COMMENT #161: The reason I "*lump*" the so-called "*conservative eclectic scholars*" with the so-called "*radical eclectic scholars*" is that they both worship the Westcott and Hort (Nestle/Aland, United Bible Societies, Critical Text) of the Vatican ("B") and Sinai ("Aleph") manuscripts in place of those that follow the Traditional Received Text. This is the same text as that used by the Roman Catholic Church, the liberal modernists, and the neo-evangelicals. It is a mystery to me as to why such Fundamentalist separatists would want to join hands in textual matters with such people. As I have mentioned before, neither of these groups is genuinely "*eclectic*," but they both follow the extremely narrow group of manuscripts which follow the Vatican-wolf-manuscript which is dressed up like a sheep.

While we are on the "*lumping*" subject, why do these writers and their employer, Bob Jones University, lump together all those people who stand for the King James Bible and its underlying Hebrew, Aramaic, and Greek **Words**? Why do they do that?

> Why to the "*lump*" me, the BIBLE FOR TODAY, and the Dean Burgon Society and others like us in with Peter Ruckman and his Ruckmanite followers? We do not agree with his position on the King James Bible and many other things.

"Doubts" of "Faith and Doctrine"

STATEMENT #162: (p. 163) [quoting Philip Mauro with approval] "*(2) that the sum of all the variant readings taken together does not give ground for the slightest doubt as to any of the fundamental points of faith and doctrine. In other words the very worse text that could be constructed from the abundant materials available would not disturb any of the great truths of the Christian faith.*"

COMMENT #162: These writers and Bob Jones University that employs them are quoting Mauro with approval. His statement is a blatant falsehood! Once again, as I have done in earlier pages of this book, I invite the reader to get a copy and study Dr. Jack Moorman's 100-page documentation on *356 Doctrinal Passages in the NIV and Its Underlying Greek Text* (BFT #2956 @ $10 + $4 S&H). These 356 doctrinal passages do indeed bring the "*slightest doubt*" and "*disturb*" some of the "*fundamental points of faith and doctrine*" and some of the "*great truths of the Christian faith.*" How many times are these Bob Jones University staff members, and others who follow them, going to repeat this lie and falsehood? They should know better by now. I have warned them about this in all of my recent books: (1) *Fundamentalist Distortions on Bible Versions* (BFT #2928 @ $7.00 + $3 S&H), (2)

Fundamentalist Misinformation on Bible Versions (**BFT #2974** @ $7.00 + $3 S&H), (3) *Fundamentalist Deception on Bible Preservation* (**BFT #3234** @ $8.00 + $3.00 S&H), and others.

"Doctrinal Changes" Do "Result"

STATEMENT #163: (p. 163) *"If the most liberal of the critical eclectic scholars set out to begin an anti-KJV conspiracy group and consistently chose the <u>worst possible readings</u> from his alternatives, <u>no doctrinal changes would result</u>."*

COMMENT #163: This is a repetition of a blatant falsehood! Let me say once more, as I have done in just the preceding STATEMENT #162 and in the earlier pages of this book, I invite the reader to get a copy and study Dr. Jack Moorman's 100-page documentation on *356 Doctrinal Passages in the NIV and Its Underlying Greek Text* (**BFT #2956** @ $10 + $5 S&H).

In my book, *Defending the King James Bible* (**BFT#1594** @ $12.00 + $5 S&H), Chapter five, I have listed 158 of those 356 doctrinal passages showing the false doctrines involved in each passage. I cannot understand how these Bob Jones University staff men can be so ignorant of these 356 doctrinal passages. Or, if they are cognizant of these passages, I am truly amazed that they cannot see these passages do involve *"<u>doctrinal changes</u>."* Where is their theological fundamentalism if they cannot see that these changes affect sound doctrine?

No "Inspired English Wording"

STATEMENT #164: (p. 163) *"While the <u>exact inspired English wording</u> sounds comforting, God expects study, comparing thoughts, and preaching with Scripture. . . ."*

COMMENT #164: We do not have any *"<u>inspired English Wording</u>."* This is a false charge. I and my fellow defenders of the King James Bible do not take this position.

God's verbal plenary inspiration is only at the level of the Hebrew, Aramaic, and Greek <u>Words</u>.

STATEMENT #165: (p. 164) *"The various KJV only views on the <u>preservation of Scripture</u> do not contradict Scripture, but neither are they <u>proved from Scripture</u>."*

COMMENT #165: I believe my view of the *"<u>preservation of Scripture</u>"* is also *"<u>proved from Scripture</u>."* My view of Bible Preservation is supported by the Lord Jesus Christ Himself in <u>Words</u> that He repeated in three of the four Gospels: *"Heaven and earth shall pass away but my <u>Words</u> shall not pass away"* (Matthew 24:35; Mark 13:31; Luke 21:33). What more do we need? That certainly is the preservation of every one of the Hebrew, Aramaic, and Greek <u>Words</u> of the original Bible.

Matthew 5:18 is further proof of God's promise to preserve even the smallest Hebrew letter, the *yodh*, and even the smallest vowel point (the "tittle") of the Hebrew text. By extension, this applies to the New Testament <u>Words</u> as well.

Not "Committing Heresy"

STATEMENT #166: (p. 164) *"Unfortunately, some KJV advocates in their zeal to promote <u>**their own view as the only correct one**</u>, castigate all other views as false. Some go so far as to <u>**accuse those who disagree of heresy**</u> or doctrinal error. However, by so doing they themselves are <u>**committing the heresy**</u> of divisive factionalism as condemned in 1 Corinthians 11:18-19."*

COMMENT #166: If our view is true and God has indeed preserved the Hebrew, Aramaic, and Greek <u>Words</u> which underlie our King James Bible and the translation is accurate, then why should we not promote our view as "<u>*the only correct one*</u>." It is especially proper since the other versions have the wrong underlying <u>Words</u> and are inaccurate in their translations.

We cannot pick up the New American Standard Version and say it is an accurate translation from the proper Hebrew, Aramaic, and Greek <u>Words</u>. They use improper Hebrew <u>Words</u> and improper Greek <u>Words</u>. It is a phony translation. It is a mistranslation in over 4,000 places from my actual count. Neither can you say that about the NIV.

These men are wrong and we are right. Their position is false and ours is true. This is what we say. Truth is the dividing line.

I never call anyone a "<u>*heretic*</u>" just because he disagrees with me. I do call those who are theological heretics, "<u>*theological heretics*</u>" such as Bishop Westcott and Professor Hort. These men were "<u>*heretics*</u>." You have never heard me call a Fundamentalist a "<u>*heretic*</u>." I may call some of the Fundamentalists' views "<u>*heretical*</u>." I may call some Fundamentalists' positions heretical positions. That doesn't make THEM "<u>*heretics*</u>." I have never said that.

STATEMENT #167: (p. 165) [Speaking of James White] *"As Pickering unfairly lumped the <u>**eclectic positions,**</u> White falls into the common pitfall of unfairly grouping the <u>**non-eclectic positions**</u>."*

COMMENT #167: What's the problem with so-called "*non-eclectic positions*"? In the first place, the so-called "*eclectic positions*" are not really "*eclectic*" but rely principally upon the Vatican manuscript ("B"). The so-called "*non-eclectic positions*" are really more "*eclectic*" than those who use the name of "*eclectic*" because they found their positions upon over 99% of the Greek New Testament manuscripts rather than on just the Vatican and a few of those that agree with it.

The Bible Not "A Minor Issue"

STATEMENT #168: (p. 165) *"The KJV Only proponents must temper their tendency toward strife over a minor issue. . . . Christians espousing their KJV Only view should protect themselves over the charge of heresy by not majoring on minor issues."*

COMMENT #168: I do not intend to "*temper*" my stand for the King James Bible and its underlying preserved original Hebrew, Aramaic, and Greek **Words** that underlie it. Is there anything more major than what is your Bible? If there is, I don't know of anything that is more major doctrinally important than what your Bible is. To tear to shreds these **Words** as this Bob Jones University book does is inexcusable. That is what this present book does in part. That is what Bob Jones University does in its Greek department. That is what Detroit Baptist Seminary does in its Greek department. That is what Central Baptist Seminary does in its Greek department. That is what Calvary Baptist Seminary does in its Greek department. These schools favor another Greek text in their New Testament that is different from the Traditional Text underlying the King James Bible in over 8,000 exact differences. See Dr. Jack Mormon's book for these differences **(BFT #3084 @ $65.00 + $7.50 S&H)**.

> It is not a "*minor issue.*" It is a major issue indeed. For these Bob Jones University authors to level a charge of "*heresy*" at those of us who stand strong for these matters is misuse of the term and total falsehood.

CHAPTER 9
COMPARING THEORIES

STATEMENT #169: (p. 171) [From Chapter Nine, "Comparing Theories"] *"The seven criteria for evaluating theories follow. Any theory of textual criticism must satisfy these tests. 1. Biblical . . . 2. Coherent . . . 3. Adequate . . . 4. Consistent . . . 5. Accurate . . . 6. Simple . . . 7. Fruitful . . ."*

COMMENT #169: Every one of these *"seven criteria"* apply completely to the <u>Words</u> underlying the King James Bible.

Erasmus Not the Source of the KJV

STATEMENT #170: (p. 177) [They are talking about the Textus Receptus] *"DEFINITION: The <u>original reading is to be found in Erasmus's edition</u> of the Greek New Testament (based on manuscripts providentially provided by God <u>to prepare the way for the KJV</u>)."*

COMMENT #170: To say that the *"<u>original reading</u>"* of the Textus Receptus *"<u>is to be found in Erasmus's edition</u>* is totally and completely false. The Latin words, *"<u>Textus Receptus</u>,"* mean *"received text,"* or that text of the Greek New Testament that has been received from church history dating back to the original writings of that text in the first century A.D.

> **The wording of these writers implies that the *"<u>Textus Receptus</u>"* began with Erasmus in 1516, when in fact it began in the time of the Apostles. Erasmus simply put these <u>Words</u> that had been received from Apostolic times into movable type for the first time. But the <u>Words</u> he put in type were the <u>Words</u> passed down through the ages from Paul, Peter, and the other Apostles.**

The second lie is to be found in the words that the *"<u>Erasmus's edition</u>"* was used *"<u>to prepare the way for the KJV</u>."* This implies that that edition was somehow the basis for the King James Bible. Why don't these men know that the King James Bible was not based on the Erasmus Greek text of 1516, but on Beza's 5th edition 1598, eighty-two years later? When are they going to get this thing straight? Do they need some more degrees? It seems to me that anybody who knows the facts would be able to understand it. Erasmus is not the foundation and the beginning of the Textus Receptus, nor is Erasmus' Greek Text the basic foundational Greek Text of our King James Bible. The Textus Receptus has been around since Apostolic times, and did not originate with Erasmus in 1516.

KJV Not the "Inspired Text"

STATEMENT #171: (p. 178) [They are talking about the KJV Only theory] *"DEFINITION: <u>the inspired text</u> is precisely that found in the English translation known as <u>the King James Version</u>."*

COMMENT #171: I do not believe that the King James Bible is the *"<u>inspired text</u>."* Yet I am falsely and willfully lumped together as one who believes this serious error, which I do not believe. My name is listed in the book right after that of *"<u>Peter S. Ruckman</u>."* As I have mentioned many times before in this study, the King James Bible is the only accurate English translation from the preserved inspired original Hebrew, Aramaic, and Greek **Words** that underlie it--but it is not "*inspired*" in any correct sense of that term, that is, "*God-breathed.*"

STATEMENT #172: (pp. 178-79) [they are still referring to the KJV Only group] "WEAKNESSES: *It rejects importance of the original Greek of the* **autographs***; it ignores* **manuscript evidence***; treats the translation as* **original document***; accepts commonly recognized interpolations such as the Comma Johanneum in spite of evidence. . . .*"

COMMENT #172: This is a scurrilous attempt to blacken the names and character of every person who stands for the King James Bible and its underlying **Words** under the name of "*King James Only.*" This is why I despise that term.

> I do not reject the Greek "*autographs.*" I do not ignore "*manuscript evidence.*" I do not treat any translation as an "*original document.*" I do not say the Johanine Comma is an "*interpolation*" but is correctly put in our King James Bible.

Christ Did Not Quote From the LXX

STATEMENT #173: (p. 179) [talking about the KJV Only group] "*. . . foreign languages weakly addressed; ignores Christ's example of using both original Hebrew and a translation (***Septuagint***).*"

COMMENT #173: This is totally false. The Lord Jesus Christ did not quote from the "*Septuagint.*" How could he quote from something that was not even in existence in the Lord Jesus Christ's days on earth?

> There is no evidence that the complete Genesis through Malachi in Greek was in existence B.C., only a few parts of it. The first complete Old Testament in Greek is found in the fifth column of Origen's six-column Hexapla. He lived in the 200's A.D. and not B.C. No man living or dead has ever proved that the entire Old Testament from Genesis to Malachi was translated from Hebrew into the Greek language B.C.

A few books were there in the Greek language B.C., but not the entire Old Testament. To say that the Lord Jesus quoted from it is false.

STATEMENT #174: (p. 179) "*Critical Eclecticism is more objective, but still permits conjectural emendation.* **Conservative eclecticism** *recognizes that the rest of* **Scripture** *is preserved in total in the* **mass of manuscripts***.*"

COMMENT #174: This is a twist of the truth. According to the so-called "*conservative eclecticism*" such as practiced by these two authors and Bob Jones University that they represent, "*Scripture*" is preserved in the Vatican and Sinai manuscript tradition and not in the "*mass of manuscripts*" at all.

STATEMENT #175: (p. 180) [There is a chart labeled "Theories of Textual Transmission." They have under the Textus Receptus the following "*disadvantage*"] "*Must apply logic of faith to Erasmus' text even when it differs from most manuscripts.*"

COMMENT #175: I remind my readers once again that the Erasmus' text of 1516 is not the Beza's 5th edition, 1598 (eighty-two years later) from which the Textus Receptus was translated.

> There are very few instances where Beza's Greek text "*differs from most manuscripts*," and in these cases the truth is corroborated by either early versions or quotations from the early church fathers.

Christ Did Not "Quote" From the LXX

STATEMENT #176: (p. 181) "*The King James Only position fails the test of accuracy. The position that only one text can be current (traditional) at a time is simply inaccurate when compared to Christ's example of quoting from both the Hebrew and the Septuagint.*"

COMMENT #176: As I mentioned before, this is a lie. The Lord Jesus Christ could not have quoted from the Greek Old Testament, the "*Septuagint,*" when it was not even in existence until the 200's A.D. long after He was on the earth.

> As all of the Jews of His day, the Lord Jesus Christ used and quoted only from the "*Hebrew*" Old Testament.

Statements on Unit III
Translation of Scripture

"Preserved" Only "Word" Not "Words"

STATEMENT #177:   (p. 185) [From Unit #III "Translation of Scripture"] *"You now have the necessary background to understand issues concerning Bible translations. You have seen that <u>God has preserved His word</u> . . . ."*

   COMMENT #177: Here again these authors are referring to God's "<u>Word</u>" instead of God's "<u>Words</u>." By this term they believe that God has preserved only His "*ideas, thoughts, concepts, message, truth, or teachings,*" rather than the original Hebrew, Aramaic, and Greek <u>Words</u>. They do not even know what the Bible is that He has "*<u>preserved</u>*."

> **The Bible that God has "*<u>preserved</u>*" consists of the original Hebrew, Aramaic, and Greek <u>Words</u>. That is the original Bible.**

   These authors and the Bob Jones University they represent do not believe God has "*<u>preserved</u>*" His <u>Words</u>. This belief is a serious apostasy and heresy. In this area, they are no better than the Roman Catholics, the modernist apostates, or the neo-evangelicals. It is a shame!

   [I have made no comments on Chapter 10, "The Translators to the Reader"]

CHAPTER 11
TRANSLATION
PRINCIPLES AND ISSUES
Modern Versions Close to W&H Greek

STATEMENT #178:   (p. 247) [From Chapter 11, "Translation Principles and Issues"] *"Almost without exception, modern translations reflect the text closer to the <u>1881 Greek text which Westcott and Hort edited</u> than to the Textus Receptus which Desiderius Erasmus edited in 1522. Since the Textus Receptus is the basis of our beloved King James Version, every English version* *based on the Westcott and Hort Greek text will naturally share differences from the KJV at these points.*"

COMMENT #178:

First of all, these writers admit that the modern versions are very close to the "*1881 Greek text* [of] *Westcott and Hort.*" This is a very important admission, because many of the modern Critical Text worshipers seek to completely divorce their present Greek texts form Westcott and Hort.

When these writers say that the Textus Receptus was "*edited*" by Erasmus in 1522, it sounds like he invented this text and that it therefore **began** with him. This is a totally false inference. This was the traditional Greek text that had been handed down from Apostolic times to the present. It did not **begin** in 1516 or even 1522 in the days of Erasmus.

"Doctrine" Is "Affected"

STATEMENT #179: (p. 247) "*In spite of all the uproar, our first five chapters stressed that these differences affect very few passages, and never affect doctrine.*"

COMMENT #179: Both of these statements are entirely false.

(1) In the first place, "*these differences*" in the two Greek texts are sizeable. In the New Testament, Dr. Jack Moorman has outlined over 8,000 differences between the Greek Text of Nestle/Aland and the Greek Text underlying the King James Bible.

This research is a result of hundreds of hours of research. It gives the Greek **Words** and the English translations. His book of over 500-large-pages on "*8,000 Differences between the NIV and Modern Versions and the Words Underlying the King James Bible*" is available from the BIBLE FOR TODAY for a gift of **$65.00 + $7.50 S&H**. It is **BFT #3084**.

(2) In the second place, it is a total lie to say that "*these differences*" can "*never affect doctrine.*" Once again I invite the reader to get a copy and study Dr. Jack Moorman's 100-page documentation on *356 Doctrinal Passages in the NIV and Its Underlying Greek Text* (BFT #2956 @ $10 + $4 S&H).

Dr. Moorman has gone through each doctrinal passage from Matthew through Revelation to show these 356 passages where false doctrine appears in the Critical Text.

When is Bob Jones University and their staff members going to cease writing about and telling these lies to their readers and students? I think it is about time they begin telling the truth in both of these areas. Their ignorance of the truth is no excuse for their continuation in falsehoods. I was under the impression that Fundamentalist institutions like Bob Jones University and their staff members were not supposed to lie since lying is of the Devil who is the father of lies (John 8:44). Am I wrong about this?

STATEMENT #180: (p. 248) *"Most of us have heard that the word conversation is used in the KJV means conduct or lifestyle. Did the KJV translators mess up? Not at all, if you check the Old English dictionary to see what the word conversation meant in 1611, you find that its meaning at that time included the manner of lifestyle."*

COMMENT #180: They are trying to say that some of the King James Bible's language is outdated. This is why the BIBLE FOR TODAY has published the *Defined King James Bible* where uncommon words are defined accurately in the footnotes. See http://www.biblefortoday.org/kj_bibles.asp for more information on how to order a copy. If a person had a copy of this Bible, he or she would not have any excuse for throwing away the King James Bible and accepting some of the modern versions which are filled with both textual and translational errors. Some have a small dictionary of uncommon words in the KJB to look them up, but it saves time to have them right on the page where they are found such as in the *Defined King James Bible*.

STATEMENT #181: (p. 249) *"The current edition of the KJV dates from 1769 and is not as difficult (due to extensive spelling corrections and <u>corrections</u> of wording <u>in at least eight passages</u>)."*

COMMENT #181: This is a quotation from James White.

For a change, it is partially true. The King James Bible is not as difficult because of these spelling changes and the change from Gothic to German script. I doubt what he said about "*<u>corrections</u>*" in "*<u>at least eight passages</u>*."

STATEMENT #182: (p. 249) *"This reflects a tendency for such <u>words to narrow in meaning</u> from general to specific over time in living languages. (Other examples include present, study, and published)."*

COMMENT #182: To find out the present "<u>meanings</u>" of uncommon words, the reader should get a copy of the *Defined King James Bible* which is published by The BIBLE FOR TODAY. If you have this Bible you will not be in doubt as to what any of the uncommon words mean. As I mentioned earlier, you can find out the various varieties of this Bible at http://www.biblefortoday.org/kj_bibles.asp if you wish to get a copy for yourself. You can also check out the ad for this Bible in the Order Blank pages just before the back cover of this book.

"Continue to Use" the KJV

STATEMENT #183: (p. 250) *"Two responses are possible. One is to <u>continue to use</u> the time-tested and beautiful poetic language of the KJV and to simply keep in mind that words like 'conversation' and 'corn' <u>that have changed meaning</u>."*

        COMMENT #183: By all means born-again Christians should "*<u>continue to use</u>*" the King James Bible. If they have difficulty in understanding some of the uncommon words, they could get one of our *Defined King James Bibles* which have, in the footnotes, accurate definitions of these words "*<u>that have changed meaning</u>*."

Not Just "A Few Dozen Differences"

STATEMENT #184: (p. 250) [This is found in the section "*What is Translating*"] *"<u>Greek manuscripts are not the main cause of differences</u> among translations, and even language development accounts for <u>only a few dozen differences</u>. The primary reason for differences among versions is that the translators themselves hold to <u>different philosophies of translation</u> and use different methods to achieve different purposes in their translations."*

        COMMENT #184: (p. 250) This is a blatant lie that different Greek manuscripts account for "<u>only a few dozen differences</u>." In the New Testament, Dr. Jack Moorman has outlined <u>over 8,000 differences</u> between the Greek Text of Nestle/Aland and the Greek Text underlying the King James Bible. It is a result of hundreds of hours of research. It gives the Greek <u>Words</u> and the English translations. This book of over 500-large-pages on "*8,000 Differences between the NIV and Modern Versions and the <u>Words</u> Underlying the King James Bible*" is available from the BIBLE FOR TODAY for a gift of **$65.00 + $7.50 S&H.** It is **BFT #3084.** There are hundreds and hundreds of differences, not "*<u>only a few dozen differences</u>*." There are 356 doctrinal passages alone are to be found in these differences. Once again I invite the reader to get a copy and study Dr. Jack Moorman's 100-page documentation on *356 Doctrinal Passages in the NIV and Its Underlying Greek Text* **(BFT #2956 @ $10 + $4 S&H).**

The writers are correct in saying that there are "*different philosophies of translation*." The King James Bible translators believed in using verbal equivalence by bringing the Hebrew, Aramaic, and Greek <u>Words</u> into English as clearly as possible. They also believed in formal equivalence. That is, wherever possible, they brought the forms of the Hebrew, Aramaic, and Greek <u>Words</u> into the same forms in English. That is, nouns were brought over as nouns, verbs as verbs, and so on. That is not the case in the modern versions such as the NASV, the NIV, the RSV, the NRSV and many of the others. They use dynamic equivalence. That means they add to the <u>Words</u> of Hebrew, Aramaic, and Greek, and subtract from those <u>Words</u>, or change those <u>Words</u> in some other way. This is a serious travesty and cannot honestly be called "*translation.*"

STATEMENT #185: (p. 255) "*A translation, then, is a conversion of meaning* (not just sounds) from one language into another in light of the vocabulary, grammar, and syntax of both languages."

COMMENT #185: I do not think "*translation*" has to do with mere "*meaning.*" It must be a "*translation*" of the precise Hebrew, Aramaic, and Greek <u>Words</u>, not just any "*meaning*" at all. In John 3:16, ("*For God so loved the world, that he gave his only begotten Son, that whosoever believeth in him should not perish, but have everlasting life.*") this is not merely a translation of whatever "*meaning*" the translator wants to place on it. It is a translation of the <u>Words</u> in that verse.

The word "*translate*" comes from two Latin words, TRANS ("*across*") and LATUS (the past participle of FERO, meaning "*to carry*"). So TRANSLATUS means "*to carry across*" from one language to another. The <u>Words</u> of Hebrew, Aramaic, and Greek are to be "*carried across*" from those languages into all the languages of the world. This has been done accurately in our King James Bible. They did not convert merely the "*meaning,*" but the <u>Words</u> from one language to English. Every <u>Word</u> has its "*meaning,*" but the translation is not a translation of meaning, but a translation of <u>Words</u>. Those <u>Words</u> are what give the verses their "*meaning.*" There is an important distinction between "*Word translation*" and "*meaning translation*" and the modern versions err in this area.

"NASB" Not "Literal Translation"

STATEMENT #186: (p. 256) [speaking of "*literal translation*"] ". . . they lack opportunity to explain or interpret what they think it means. The *KJV and the NASB are examples of this type of translation.*"

COMMENT #186: This is absolutely false. The term "*literal translation*" does not belong to the "*NASB*" (New American Standard Version). It does belong to the King James Bible. The King James Bible is both a literal and a literary translation at the same time.

In my analysis of the New American Standard Version from Genesis through Revelation (BFT #1494 @ $15.00+$5.00 S&H), I found over 4,000 examples where the NASV is not a literal translation. This is a comparison of the Hebrew, Aramaic, and Greek. These 4,000 examples either added to the Words of God, subtracted from the Words of God, or changed the Words of God in some other way.

This is sin. It is a blatant lie to claim the NASV is literal. The King James Bible is literal and accurate. The New American Standard Version is not accurate or literal in over 4,000 places.

We Need More Than "Meaning"

STATEMENT #187: (p. 256) "*In contrast, idiomatic translations attempt to communicate the meaning in natural English.*"

COMMENT #187: That is the problem "*communicating the meaning.*" You must translate the Words and each Word has a "*meaning.*" We have to communicate not simply the "*meaning,*" but the Words, which are vitally important indeed. The so-called "*idiomatic translations*" fail to do this.

Many "Doctrinal Variations"

STATEMENT #188: (p. 263) "*We have already shown that no doctrinal variations arise regardless of which manuscripts are used. Thus choice of manuscripts cannot result in a theological biased translation. Bias from Greek sources can only come from frequent use of conjectural emendation.*"

COMMENT #188: Again the writers, and Bob Jones University that employs them have been guilty of a blatant falsehood. Once again I invite the reader to get a copy and study Dr. Jack Moorman's 100-page documentation on *356 Doctrinal Passages in the NIV and Its Underlying Greek Text* (BFT #2956 @ $10 + $4 S&H). There are 356 passages where "*doctrinal variations arise*" due to the false Critical Text that is used either of Westcott and Hort, Nestle-Aland, or United Bible Societies. These false texts are based on the false manuscripts of the Vatican ("B") and the Sinai ("Aleph").

"Theological Bias" and "Manuscripts"

STATEMENT #189: (p. 264) "*We have argued that theological bias does not depend either on selection of manuscripts or on translation of a few sample passages.*"

COMMENT #189: Theological bias **does** depend on a "*selection of manuscripts.*" The Vatican ("B") and Sinai ("Aleph") "*manuscripts*" originated with the Gnostics of Alexandria, Egypt. Alexandria was the headquarters of Gnosticism.

> As Dean John W. Burgon has pointed out, when the Gnostics of Egypt, and other heretical groups, failed to find Scripture verses to back up their false teachings, they changed the Scripture verses to conform to their teachings.

That is the cause of doctrinal impurity in the Westcott and Hort text and other Critical Texts.

CHAPTER 12

SELECTING VERSIONS

We "Need to Get Overly Concerned"

STATEMENT #190: (p.270) [From Chapter Twelve, "Selecting Versions"] "*Most differences among Bible versions in English are due to issues over how words should be translated rather than which manuscripts are the best. This means that a person buying a Bible need not get overly concerned about those issues.*"

COMMENT #190: I think both of these things must be considered. Corrupt "*manuscripts*" are very much a part of this issue. Corrupt manuscripts are where you get into these 356 doctrinal passages that Dr. Jack Moorman has catalogued **(BFT #2956 @ $10 + $4 S&H)**. People should be "*concerned*" about both the **Words** used and the techniques of translation. They should keep their King James Bible to insure the proper **Words** and accurate translation technique. These two end up with proper theology. Do not use these modern versions, which are trying to make merchandise of the **Words** of God. They have failed as far as accuracy of translation is concerned. They have failed as far as the proper Hebrew, Aramaic, and Greek **Words**, which underlie it.

> The fourfold superiority of our King James Bible is found in my book, *Defending the King James Bible* **(BFT #1594 @ $12.00+$5.00 S&H)**. It is over 350 pages in hardback edition and is in its 9th printing. It proves the King James Bible to be superior in four areas: (1) superior in the texts of Hebrew, Aramaic, and Greek; (2) superior in translators; (3) superior in translation technique; and (4) superior in theology.

It can be ordered by calling **1-800-John 10:9** or by writing BIBLE FOR

TODAY, 900 Park Avenue, Collingswood, NJ 08108.

STATEMENT #191: (p. 270) *"We have said that the key issue is not manuscript theory but translation philosophy. Literal translations stick as closely to the text as possible, while idiomatic translations and paraphrases interpret the meaning as well."*

COMMENT #191: Both *"manuscript theory"* and *"translation philosophy"* are vitally important. The King James Bible has both the proper *"manuscript theory"* and the *"translation philosophy."*

"NASB" Not "Literal"

STATEMENT #192: (p. 271) *"People who find the King James Version difficult to read or understand may want a more modern translation as a primary study Bible or as a secondary Bible to supplement their KJV. The most literal modern translation is the NASB, which stays as close to its Greek manuscript base as the KJV does."*

COMMENT #192: This is totally false. It does not even stick closely to its own Old Testament Hebrew and Aramaic **Words** or to its own New Testament Greek **Words**. As I mentioned before, it departs from the Hebrew, Aramaic and Greek **Words** over 4,000 times. On the other hand, the King James Bible sticks extremely closely to its Hebrew, Aramaic, and Greek **Words**. I do not see how these Bob Jones University staff men could be so ignorant of the truth about the **real** comparison between the NASV and the King James Bible.

> As for the KJB being *"difficult to read or understand,"* the King James Bible is on the average at a 7th grade reading level which is a lower *"reading level"* than the six other modern versions compared in *The Comparative Readability of the Authorized Version* (BFT #2671 @ $6.00 + $2.00 S&H).

The versions that in most instances were at a slightly higher reading level than the King James Bible were the NASV, NIV, RSV, NRSV, NKJV, and ASV. Do not listen to people who might tell you that the King James Bible is too difficult.

Beware of Your "Bible Study" Tools

STATEMENT #193: (p. 272) *"Unfortunately, alternative translations are too often neglected as a tool for Bible study. Whatever you prefer as your main study Bible, consider owning a KJV, an NASB, and an NKJV as reference tools."*

COMMENT #193: Why would you have the NASV or even the NKJV as *"a tool for Bible study"*? I have mentioned earlier that the

NASV has <u>over 4,000 examples</u> of either adding, subtracting, or changing in some other way the <u>Words</u> of Hebrew, Aramaic, or Greek (**Cf. BFT #1494 @ $15.00+$5.00 S&H**). Why should I trust that version as "*a tool for Bible study*"? I have made a similar study on the New King James Version (**Cf. BFT #1442 @ $10.00+$5.00 S&H**). I found in the NKJV <u>over 2,000 examples</u> of either adding, subtracting or changing in some other way the <u>Words</u> of Hebrew, Aramaic, or Greek. Why should I trust that version as "*a tool for Bible study*"? Stick to the King James Bible and its underlying Hebrew, Aramaic, and Greek <u>Words</u> as your only safe "*tools for Bible study*."

Need More Than to "Communicate"

STATEMENT #194: (p. 273) "*We have already argued that God desires to communicate. He used common Greek rather than formal classical Greek for the New Testament.*"

    COMMENT #194: It is not enough that God desires to "*communicate*." He also desired to have his Hebrew, Aramaic, and Greek <u>Words</u> preserved for ever. The word "*communicate*" is entirely too general a concept. It blends in with the authors' doctrine of only "*ideas, thoughts, concepts, message, truth, or teachings*" being preserved rather than the very <u>Words</u>. It is a weak and insufficient position.

"Messed Up" Children & Adults

STATEMENT #195: (p. 273) "*How do you help a child read on his own? The child will not be 'messed up' by a modern version or even a paraphrase.*"

    COMMENT #195: I deny this completely. I believe a "*child*" might be just as "*messed up*" as any adult would be when having to deal with the following facts:

> **(1) 356 doctrinal passages that are in error;**
>
> **(2) 2,886 <u>Words</u> that are missing from the New Testament;**
>
> **(3) 8,000 differences in the Greek New Testament text;**
>
> **(4) depending on the New King James, the New American Standard, or the New International Versions mistranslations by either adding, subtracting, or changing in some other ways over 2,000, 4,000, or 6,658 places respectively.**

This indeed will lead to "*messed up*" people regardless of their ages.

"Reading Level" False Charges

STATEMENT #196:   (p. 273) *"A Christian parent hearing this symptom should remedy the situation with a Bible aimed at his __reading level__."*

COMMENT #196: What these Bob Jones University staff members are trying to suggest is to get a modern version with a supposed lower *"__reading level__."*

> The King James Bible is on the average at a 7ᵗʰ grade reading level which is in many instances at a lower *"__reading level__"* than the six other modern versions compared in *The Comparative Readability of the Authorized Version* (BFT #2671 @ $6.00 + $2.00 S&H).

The versions that in most instances were at a slightly higher reading level than the King James Bible were the NASV, NIV, RSV, NRSV, NKJV, and ASV. Do not listen to people who might tell you that the King James Bible is too difficult. Some people are saying that the King James Bible is at the *"__reading level__"* of a sophomore in college. That was in an article in *Moody Monthly* published by the Moody Bible Institute. That is seriously in error. People do not have to change from the King James Bible to get an optimum or lower *"__reading level__."*

STATEMENT #197:   (p. 274) *"We've already indicated that the New International Version is a poor choice for a study Bible for an adult, however, its weaknesses are not significant for a __child's level of understanding__ and it can be used with benefit for children in junior high. Even the Living Bible, though poorer than the NIV, can even be used with young children."*

COMMENT #197:   As I mentioned in the previous statement, in most instances the NIV is not at an average lower *"__reading level__"* than the King James Bible. Why would these writers suggest that Junior High students should use either the NIV or the Living Version, both of which are loaded with so many dynamic equivalent examples?

"Antiquated" But "Accurate"

STATEMENT #198:   (pp. 274-75) [They are talking about Bibles for evangelism] *"The Christian only compounds the __difficulty of understanding__ Scripture by relating God's __Word__ in language that is __antiquated__, and the use of such languages encourages some people to pass the Bible off as __antiquated__ and __irrelevant__ for today's society."*

COMMENT #198:

One way of overcoming any "*difficulty of understanding*" is to get a copy of "*The Defined King James Bible.*" In this way, they can understand the uncommon words while at the same time get an accurate translation based upon accurate and preserved Hebrew, Aramaic, and Greek <u>Words</u>. The King James Bible is not "*irrelevant*" but accurate and clear. It is far better to have very few "*antiquated*" words, which are accurately translated, than modern words which are often mistranslated and which have an erroneous original language base with 356 erroneous doctrinal passages in their New Testaments.

Use Only the KJB For the "Gospel"

STATEMENT #199: (p. 275) "*Consider using a modern language version for witnessing or helping new converts. . . .*

Many families own a King James heirloom, but modern versions have also become very popular. . . .

. . . can we not become as an American (rather than an Elizabethan Englishman) and put version preferences aside for the sake of the <u>Gospel</u>?"

COMMENT #199: There is nothing wrong with the "<u>Gospel</u>" in the King James Bible. As a matter of fact, I prefer it to the so-called "<u>Gospel</u>" of the modern versions such as the NIV, the NASV, or the English Standard Version. Let me give you a "<u>Gospel</u>" verse and you tell me which is the "<u>Gospel</u>" and which is the false and heretical "<u>Gospel</u>"?

The verse is John 6:47 where the Lord Jesus said as translated in our King James Bible: "*Verily, verily, I say unto you, he that believeth <u>on me</u> hath everlasting life.*"

The NIV reads: "*I tell you the truth, <u>he who believes has everlasting life</u>.*" Is this the "<u>Gospel</u>"?

The NASV reads: "*Truly, truly, I say to you, <u>he who believes has everlasting life</u>.*" Is this the "<u>Gospel</u>"?

These last two versions do not give the "<u>Gospel</u>" here. According to their rendering (based on the false Westcott and Hort Greek text), you could "<u>*believe*</u>" in Atheism, Hinduism, Taoism, Muhamadanism, Judaism, Roman Catholicism, Communism, or anything you want to "<u>*believe*</u>" in and still have "<u>*everlasting life*</u>." This makes provision for a false "<u>Gospel</u>."

STATEMENT #200: (pp. 275-76) "*Others, however, prefer to let church members <u>choose their own versions</u> and provide for congregational reading by displaying the passage to be read using an <u>overhead projector</u>.*"

COMMENT #200: Is that what you want in your church?

> **Do you want your Bibles replaced with an overhead projector?**

It seems to me that if this is done, the person in the pew would not be able to follow the preaching in his own Bible. I feel that a local church should be united about its Bible version so they would be able to read the Bible in unison without a cacophony. Our 𝕭ible 𝕱or 𝕿oday 𝕭aptist 𝕮hurch uses and defends the King James Bible. Other churches use and defend other versions. Even though I do not concur with those other versions, it seems to me that the church attendees should be united on the version used in the church and follow along with it rather than to have a multitude of versions and therefore have to resort to an *overhead projector* to gain some semblance of temporary unity on their Bible. To say that it is all right for a local church to have a disunity on the Bible version issue, though not uncommon, is strange to me. It should not be so. It is an *"uncertain sound"* (1 Corinthians 14:8).

"Teachings" Are "Affected"

STATEMENT #201: (p. 276) [Under the section on charity] *"As the KJV advocate Philip Mauro has stated, the teachings of the New Testament are unaffected by any of the texts available to us. In light of this, we should temper our responses to those who differ over which of them to use. The Apostle Paul insisted that love [KJV--'charity'] suffereth long. . . ."*

COMMENT #201: I completely disagree with that alleged quote from Philip Mauro. These authors are agreeing with him completely on this quotation. There are at least 356 doctrinal passages where the *"teachings of the New Testament"* are affected by the Westcott and Hort kind of texts. If any one should question this, once again I invite the reader to get a copy and study Dr. Jack Moorman's 100-large-page documentation on *356 Doctrinal Passages in the NIV and Its Underlying Greek Text* (BFT #2956 @ $10 + $4 S&H).

> I do agree that *"love suffereth long."* But in the same chapter and context, Paul also reminds us that charity or love *"rejoiceth in the truth"* (1 Corinthians 13:6). I have been rejoicing in the *"truth"* of the King James Bible and its underlying Hebrew, Aramaic, and Greek <u>Words</u> ever since I learned the truth about this important subject in 1970.

I do not intend to change any of the facts, documentation, and books that I have accumulated since 1970. I have collected over 1,000 titles that defend the King James Bible and its underlying Hebrew, Aramaic, and Greek <u>Words</u>. These titles are listed in our **Brochure #1** (available upon request) and in my book, *Defending the King James Bible* in the Appendix (BFT #1594 @

$12.00+$5.00 S&H).

> The Bible is a vitally important issue. What is contained in your Bible builds your theology and your doctrines. It is vitally important that you have the right Bible for right theology and right doctrines. You cannot have these 356 doctrinal perversions found in the underlying texts of the ASV, RSV, NRSV, NASV, NIV, ESV and other modern versions and hope to have correct theology and doctrine. We cannot and must not have a love of falsity and untruth.

We must rejoice "*in the truth*" as well as have a love for the brethren, even though they differ with us. As the Bible enjoins us, we must "*Prove all things; hold fast unto that which is good*" (1 Thessalonians 5:21). I am going to continue to "*hold fast*" to the King James Bible and its underlying **Words** which I believe is "*good.*" At the same time, I will continue to have charity and love for those who differ with me on this and especially for those who have not studied the matter.

> I was asleep about this issue for about 20 years. Although I used the King James Bible, I did not know why, because I was taught at Dallas Theological Seminary for five years in the classroom, and then several years beyond that while writing my dissertations for the Master of Theology and the Doctor of Theology, that the Westcott and Hort type of Greek Text was the proper text. That was all they gave us at that Seminary and that was all they taught us. I was in the dark about that. For those who are in the dark about this subject (as I was), and that is all they know and have been taught, I have special love and desire that they will grow in knowledge like I grew. When I started to study this subject I found the facts were completely on the side of the **Words** of the Traditional Textus Receptus which underlies the King James Bible. I have changed to the Textus Receptus side and I am not turning back because it is the right view.

"Brethren" Not "Condemned"

STATEMENT #202: (p. 276) "*This contrasts sharply with the many voices that __condemn__--not clear enemies of the cross, not the liberals that deny the Gospel, or the Roman Catholics who adulterate the Gospel, or the cults who preach another Gospel, but--true believers **Christian brethren** who simply disagree with their opinions about the transmission and translation of Scripture. __The absence of love for anything but their own opinions__ is not a fruit of the Spirit.*"

COMMENT #202: I do not "*condemn Christian brethren*" as people. Where it is called for, I "*condemn*" what I consider to be their false philosophy, theology, or doctrine--and rightly so. I shall continue to do so as long as the Lord gives me breath. I do not attack their persons or their character. I rejoice that they are "*Christian brethren.*" I do, however, strongly and fervently "*condemn*" some of the positions, teachings, beliefs, and doctrines of some of my "*Christian brethren.*" The writers of this book do not seem to understand (or do not **want** to understand) the difference in these matters.

There is a decided difference between an attack and condemnation of someone's person and character and an attack and condemnation of someone's teachings, beliefs, and doctrines.

The writers indicate that there is something wrong for having an "*absence of love for anything but* [our] *own opinions.*" If our "*opinions*" are correct and true, why should we not have an "*absence of love*" for anything which is incorrect or false?

As mentioned in the previous comment, charity or love "*rejoiceth in the truth*" (1 Corinthians 13:6). The Psalmist also gives some other advice: "*Therefore I esteem all thy precepts concerning all things to be right; and I hate every false way*" (Psalm 119:128). Part of "rejoicing in the truth" is to "*hate every false way.*" This I do, whether that "*false way*" is being believed or practiced by Roman Catholicism, Religious modernistic liberalism, neoevangelicalism, neofundamentalism, or Fundamentalism. It is the "*false ways*" that I hate and detest and expose, **not** the people who walk in those "*false ways.*" And there is a world of difference between these two things which any honest and intelligent person should be able to comprehend. Since these writers are honest and intelligent, why cannot they comprehend this difference?

Yes, a part of the "*fruit of the Spirit*" (Galatians 5:22-23) is "*love,*" but "*love*" for what? As I have said before, it is not that I do not "*love*" my Christian brethren (even though they are different on their **beliefs**), but I do not "*love*" their **false teachings**. Those are the things on which we disagree. I would simply implore them to seek the truth and not follow error. I despise the false teachings of all varieties that are rampant in the age in which we live. I will continue to battle against such **false teachings.**

Every saved person has been told in Jude 1:3b to "*. . . earnestly contend for the faith which was once delivered unto the saints.*" Part of *the faith* for which we must "*earnestly contend*" is the Bible. The Bible is not the Bible for which Schnaiter, Taglapietra, or Bob Jones University who employs them contends. Their present "Bible" contains only the preserved original "*ideas, thoughts, concepts, message, truth, or teachings,*" rather than the original Words of the Hebrew, Aramaic, and Greek Words. I hate their "*false teaching*" in this area of Bible preservation! Notice I did not say I hated the "teachers" just the "false teachings."

I have shaken the hand of Sam Schnaiter on one occasion. He asked me to autograph my book, *Defending the King James Bible.* I do not dislike him or hate him. That goes for Bob Jones III as well. I know him also. I have met him and visited with him. It is some of the "*false teachings*" on the Bible which they promulgate that I despise and I will continue to despise. I will continue to have uncharitableness for the **teaching, theology, doctrines and beliefs**, which are wrong and false. All genuine Christians should do the same.

"Love Cuts Both Ways"

STATEMENT #203: (p. 276) "*Such love cuts both ways. KJV advocates must show love toward those using other versions, and those using modern versions must not scorn those using the KJV.*"

COMMENT #203: Yes, "*love cuts both ways.*" I would agree to that. It does "*cut both ways.*" As I have said before I do not have hatred toward these who differ with me on the version issue. I am strong on my criticism of their **false views**. I have hatred toward the **false views** that they share, but not for them as people. They should not say nor can they prove that I do. I never have and I never will. From the following, it would seem that those using modern versions have strong ill will if not hatred for those who stand for the King James Bible and its underlying original language Words. Notice in the FBF Resolution #01.5, they referred to Bible-believing Christians as merely "*Brethren*" in quotation marks as if to doubt their salvation.

Fundamental Baptist Fellowship Resolution #01.5:

"Resolutions from 81st Annual Meeting of the Fundamental Baptist Fellowship! Resolution Number 01.5

Regarding Schismatic "Brethren"

Sent October 3, 2001

In light of the public attacks and false accusations upon the FBF, its leaders, and other like-minded Fundamentalist institutions regarding their respective positions on the text of Scripture and translations, we reaffirm that within the historic orthodox doctrine of Bibliology these are matters of soul-liberty and should not be a test of fellowship for Fundamentalists. Since not all professors or pastors have expertise in the field of textual studies, disagreements regarding text or translation should be resolved by honest discussion as opposed to libelous contention. Those who repeatedly attempt to unnecessarily divide Fundamentalists over this issue and refuse to repent should be regarded as schismatics who must be rejected as the Word of God instructs (Romans 16:17-18; Titus 3:9-11; 1 Corinthians 3:10-17)."

This resolution from the Fundamental Baptist Fellowship certainly does not sound like *"love"* for the saved *"brethren"* who stand for the King James Bible and its underlying preserved Hebrew, Aramaic, and Greek **Words**.

Scripture Mis-Applied To "Brethren" Titus 3:9-11

[9] *"But avoid foolish questions, and genealogies, and contentions, and strivings about the law; for they are unprofitable and vain.*

[10] *A man that is an heretick after the first and second admonition reject;*

[11] *Knowing that he that is such is subverted, and sinneth, being condemned of himself."*

Where To Find "Reading Levels"

STATEMENT #204: (p. 278) *"Find the reading level for the King James Version, the New American Standard Bible, the New International Version, and the Living Bible by visiting or phoning a Christian bookstore."*

COMMENT #204: This simply will not work. *"Visiting or phoning a Christian bookstore"* will not give you your truthful answer. They just parrot what the various modern version editors tell them. To **really** find out the "_reading level_" of the KJV, ASV, RSV, NASV, NIV, NKJV, and NRSV you must get the only book in the world that I know of that has done a complete computer study on this very question, using all of the modern techniques of analysis. It is a book by our oldest son, D. A. Waite, Jr. It is entitled _The Comparative Readability of the Authorized Version_ **(BFT #2671 @ $6.00+ $2.00 S&H)**. The **Old Testament** Flesch-Kincaid **Grade Reading Level Score** (based on the Word for Windows 6 scale) is as follows:

Version	Grade Reading Level (WW6)
KJB	5.2
ASV	5.4
NIV	5.2
NRSV	5.2
RSV	5.2
NKJV	5.3
NASV	5.7

The **New Testament** Flesch-Kincaid **Grade Level Score** (based on the Word for Windows 6 scale) is as follows:

Version	Grade Reading Level (WW6)
KJB	5.2
ASV	5.3
NIV	5.2
RSV	5.3
NRSV	5.5
NKJV	5.5
NASV	5.8

These figures in this 86-page booklet are based upon the four readability indexes used even today by standard readability researchers all over the world. Though they are very close, in most areas the King James Bible is the easiest to read of the six other modern versions compared from Genesis through Revelation. On the average, the King James Bible is between a 5th and 6th grade "*reading level.*" If you ask a Christian bookstore about Bible version reading levels, they might tell you about the *Moody Monthly* report which erroneously put the King James Bible's "*reading level*" at grade 14, or that of a sophomore in college. This is a gross error, yet believed by many through ignorance of the facts.

CONCLUSION

Only "Word" Preserved, Not "Words"

STATEMENT #205: (p. 279) "*The Bible is not only inspired, but has been preserved to this day, and anyone who cares to look can see three amazing evidences of that fact that God has preserved his word since antiquity . . .*"

COMMENT #205: Here again these authors are referring to God's "**Word**" instead of God's "**Words**." By this term they believe that God has preserved only His "*ideas, thoughts, concepts, message, truth, or teachings,*" rather than the original Hebrew, Aramaic, and Greek **Words**. The authors, and Bob Jones University who pays their salary, do not believe that the **Words** of God have been "*preserved*." What kind of a "*Bible*" is this if its **Words** have not been "*preserved*"? When they use the terms "*inspired*" and "*preserved*" in the same context, one would assume that they were referring to the same kind of inspiration and preservation, that is, verbal plenary inspiration and verbal plenary preservation. But such is not the case. If these writers, and Bob Jones University that they represent, downgrade "*preservation*" only to the "*ideas, thoughts, concepts, message, truth, or teachings,*" but not the original Hebrew, Aramaic, and Greek **Words**, could you not assume that they also downgrade "*inspiration*" in the same way? Should they not be equal in kind? This is deceptive writing. They have redefined the meaning of the **Word** of God. You will never find in this book they have written that God has promised and has fulfilled that promise to "*preserve*" his original Hebrew, Aramaic, and Greek **Words**. They do not believe it. You can also take the book, *From the Mind of God to the Mind of Man*, and you will never find in there with all of the Bob Jones University-approved book written by its graduates, teachers, and consultants where they state that they believe God has preserved His original Hebrew, Aramaic, and Greek **Words**. I have answered this book in my book entitled *Fundamentalist Mis-Information on Bible Versions* (BFT #2974 @ $7.00+$3.00 S&H). You will not find this statement written in the Bob Jones University-approved sequel to that book, *God's Word in our Hands* either. I have answered that book in my book entitled *Fundamentalist Deception on Bible Preservation* (BFT #3234 @ $8.00+$3.00 S&H).

"Doctrine" & "Meaning" Affected

STATEMENT #206: (p. 279) *"Having stressed that <u>the Word of God is preserved</u>, we have attempted to delineate the issues concerning the exact wording of a small percentage of passages. <u>None of these passages affect doctrine</u> and <u>most do not even affect the meaning of the sentence</u>."*

COMMENT #206: Once again these authors are referring to God's "<u>Word</u>" instead of God's "<u>Words</u>." By this term they believe that God has preserved only His *"ideas, thoughts, concepts, message, truth, or teachings,"* rather than the original Hebrew, Aramaic, and Greek <u>Words</u>. This is deceptive. On the second point about *"<u>None of these passages affect doctrine</u>,"* I am just going to blow a trumpet on that point once again. I am going to call this teaching a lie. I am going to call it a falsehood. I am going to call it something I dislike. Once again I invite the reader to get a copy and study Dr. Jack Moorman's 100-large-page documentation on *356 Doctrinal Passages in the NIV and Its Underlying Greek Text* (BFT #2956 @ $10 + $4 S&H). Or I invite the reader to get my own book *Defending the King James Bible* (BFT #1594 @ $12.00+$5.00 S&H) and look at Chapter Five where I have listed and illustrated about 158 of these 356 passages showing that the Westcott and Hort type of Greek text does *"<u>affect doctrine</u>"* adversely. I do not understand how these highly educated brethren can make such false and misleading statements about doctrine not being affected in the Critical Text and the versions based upon it.

> To say that *"<u>none of these passages affect doctrine</u>"* is a bitter falsehood. They tell these falsehoods in order to put you at ease when you use a modern version. When you use a modern version you should not be at ease. You should be on guard. You should wonder when the new version you might be using is going to make an error, add a word here, subtract a word, eliminate a doctrine, or change a doctrine. You should not be at ease if you are reading from a modern Bible version. You should be on guard.

Better yet, you should read the King James Bible and be at ease. In that Bible, you will never find any doctrines either added, subtracted, or changed. If you do not understand some of the uncommon words, you might want to look into the possibility of getting a copy of our *Defined King James Bible* (BFT #3000, genuine leather or hardback at various prices). See http://www. biblefortoday.org/kj_bibles.asp for details if you wish to buy a copy.

As far as the statement, *<u>most do not even affect the meaning of the sentence</u>*, this is again a false statement indeed. As I have said before, in the New Testament, Dr. Jack Moorman has outlined <u>over 8,000 differences</u>

between the Greek Text of Nestle/Aland and the Greek Text underlying the King James Bible. It is a result of hundreds of hours of research. It gives the Greek words and the English translations. This book of over 500-large-pages on "*8,000 Differences between the NIV and Modern Versions and the Words Underlying the King James Bible*" is available from the BIBLE FOR TODAY for a gift of **$65.00 + $7.50 S&H**. It is BFT #3084. Many, many, though not all certainly, of these **8,000 differences** do "*affect the meaning of the sentence*."

    STATEMENT #207: (p. 279) "*We have tried to show that most of these views are within the bounds of the Christian faith and should not be tests of orthodoxy. The arguments concern tiny details in scattered passages, and no one is required to relinquish the facts of preservation outlined in the first four chapters.*"

    COMMENT #207: Do these authors and Bob Jones University that pays their salaries believe that my views **are within the bounds of the Christian faith**? It is a Biblically-based position taught by the Lord Jesus Christ Himself in several passages as mentioned earlier (Matthew 5:18-19; Matthew 24:35; Mark 13:31; and Luke 21:33). As far as the authors' so-called "*facts of preservation*," they have a seriously flawed view of "*preservation*." They only believe in the "*preservation*" of the **Word** of God, meaning only the original "*ideas, thoughts, concepts, message, truth, or teachings*," rather than the original Hebrew, Aramaic, and Greek **Words** of God. Their view is very little "*preservation*" at all.

APPENDIX 1
SCHNAITER'S
REPLY TO ACCUSATIONS
"Message" Not "Precise Wording"

    STATEMENT #208: (p. 284) [from APPENDIX 1 by Schnaiter, quoting a letter to Dr. Charles Woodbridge from his article in *Biblical Viewpoint*] "*However, the presence of manuscript variations leads us to analyze more carefully the considerations of preservation into two categories. (1) THE PRESERVATION OF THE AUTHORITATIVE MESSAGE OF GOD, and (2) THE PRESERVATION OF THE PRECISE WORDING OF THAT MESSAGE. .... However, such PROMISES OF PRESERVATION in view of the wording variations CAN ONLY APPLY TO THE MESSAGE OF GOD'S WORD, NOT TO ITS PRECISE WORDING.*"

COMMENT #208: That is a quotation from Dr. Sam Schnaiter who is Professor of New Testament Language and Literature and the Chairman of the University's Ancient Languages Department. He admits you cannot believe that God has promised and has fulfilled that promise to preserve His <u>Words</u> because there are variations. I differ completely with this quotation from the *Biblical Viewpoint* by Dr. Samuel Schnaiter on the executive teaching staff from Bob Jones University where he says, that "<u>PRESERVATION . . . CAN ONLY APPLY TO THE MESSAGE OF GOD'S WORD, NOT TO ITS PRECISE WORDING.</u>" This false position of Schnaiter and Bob Jones University is an extremely erroneous and deceptive teaching in regard to Bible "*preservation*." In fact, it is no "*preservation*" at all.

"Articles of Faith" are "Lost"

STATEMENT #209: (p. 286) [quoting Richard Bentley] "*<u>The real text of sacred writers is competently exact . . . nor is one article of faith or moral precept either perverted or lost</u>. . . . Choose as awkwardly as you will, choose <u>the worst by design</u>, out of the whole lump of readings.*"

COMMENT #209: This is a statement by Richard Bentley. Is this what these people are relying upon? He is dead wrong.

> **Who is Richard Bentley to say this falsification? His statement that you can take any text of Scripture, even <u>*the worst by design*</u>, and you will not have <u>*one article of faith or moral precept either perverted or lost*</u> does not hold up to the facts. This flies in the face of the truth.**

Once more I invite the reader to get a copy and study Dr. Jack Moorman's 100-large-page documentation on *356 Doctrinal Passages in the NIV and Its Underlying Greek Text* (BFT #2956 @ $10 + $4 S&H). This careful research proves Bentley's statement to be ridiculous and erroneous.

W&H's "Aberrations" Perpetuated

STATEMENT #210: (p. 286) "*Incidentally, the truth of it should, I would think, make rather moot the contentiousness concerning <u>Westcott and Hort's theological aberrations</u>, since they would have had <u>no opportunity to perpetuate any of them (real or imaginary) through textual criticism</u>.*"

COMMENT #210:

> **The "<u>*theological aberrations*</u>" of the apostates Westcott and Hort led them to rely upon the false manuscripts of the Vatican ("B") and Sinai ("Aleph") which themselves were loaded with doctrinal perversions and errors.**

This is the opportunity they took advantage of to "*perpetuate*" their "*theological aberrations*" upon an unsuspecting world, including the deluded world of the Fundamentalist authors of this book and Bob Jones University that employs them.

N.T. Not "Undisturbed" By Them

STATEMENT #211: (p. 286) "*My point is, therefore, that God's providential care of the New Testament is undisturbed by the manuscript variants.*"

COMMENT #211: Again this is false. The manuscripts worshiped by these authors and Bob Jones University have been perverted. They have been theologically "*disturbed*" and have over 8,000 "*manuscript variants.*"

> The providence of God was not behind the preservation of the Vatican ("B") and Sinai ("Aleph"). "*God's providential care*" was indeed "*undisturbed*" by the preserved original Hebrew, Aramaic, and Greek Words which underlie our King James Bible.

I would agree that God's providence did protect those **Words**.

"Variances" Not "Insignificant"

STATEMENT #212: (p. 287) [speaking of the King James Version] "*The variances of it from the autographs are so minute and insignificant that they are unworthy of serious discussions for the most part.*"

COMMENT #212: I do not believe that the King James Bible has any "*variances*" from "*the autographs*" because of its accurate translation of the preserved Hebrew, Aramaic, and Greek **Words** that underlie it.

They cannot say this for their favorite NASV, or the NIV, or the English Standard Version that they sell in the Bob Jones University bookstores. When they seek to do this, as they have done throughout their book, it shows how out-of-touch with reality these Bob Jones University staff men are in this area. Why are they blind to the facts on this subject? As I have often pointed out in this study, in the New Testament, Dr. Jack Moorman has outlined *over 8,000 differences* between the Greek Text of Nestle/Aland and the Greek Text underlying the King James Bible. It is a result of hundreds of hours of research. It gives the Greek words and the English translations. This book of over 500-large-pages on *8,000 Differences between the NIV and Modern Versions and the Words Underlying the King James Bible* is available from the BIBLE FOR TODAY for a gift of $65.00 + $7.50 S&H. It is **BFT #3084.** In view of this, how can these intelligent authors say the "*variations*" are *so minute and* *insignificant?* Granted, many of these **8,000** are minor, but many are anything but "*minute and insignificant.*"   I suggest these authors and Bob Jones University rush out as soon as they get this review of their book and purchase this **BFT #3084** by Dr. Jack Moorman to see how really wrong they have been in this area. It must also be pointed out that in these **8,000 differences** there are 356 doctrinal passages that are extremely vital.

> I invite the reader to get a copy and study Dr. Jack Moorman's 100-large-page documentation on *356 Doctrinal Passages in the NIV and Its Underlying Greek Text* (BFT #2956 @ $10 + $4 S&H). Each of these 356 doctrinal passages are very worthy of "*serious discussion.*"

Index of Words and Phrases

About the Author

The author of this book, Dr. D. A. Waite, received a B.A. (Bachelor of Arts) in classical Greek and Latin from the University of Michigan in 1948, a Th.M. (Master of Theology), with high honors, in New Testament Greek Literature and Exegesis from Dallas Theological Seminary in 1952, an M.A. (Master of Arts) in Speech from Southern Methodist University in 1953, a Th.D. (Doctor of Theology), with honors, in Bible Exposition from Dallas Theological Seminary in 1955, and a Ph.D. in Speech from Purdue University in 1961. He holds both New Jersey and Pennsylvania teacher certificates in Greek and Language Arts.

He has been a teacher in the areas of Greek, Hebrew, Bible, Speech, and English for over thirty-five years in ten schools, including one junior high, one senior high, three Bible institutes, two colleges, two universities, and one seminary. He served his country as a Navy Chaplain for five years on active duty; pastored two churches; was Chairman and Director of the Radio and Audio-Film Commission of the American Council of Christian Churches; since 1971, has been Founder, President, and Director of THE BIBLE FOR TODAY; since 1978, has been President of the DEAN BURGON SOCIETY; has produced over 700 other studies, books, cassettes, or VCR's on various topics; and is heard on both a five-minute daily and thirty-minute weekly radio program IN DEFENSE OF TRADITIONAL BIBLE TEXTS, on radio, shortwave, and streaming on the Internet at BibleForToday.org, 24/7/365. Dr. and Mrs. Waite have been married since 1948; they have four sons, one daughter, and, at present, eight grandchildren, and three great-grandchildren. Since October 4, 1998, he has been the Pastor of The Bible For Today Baptist Church in Collngs-wood, New Jersey.

Order Blank (p. 1)

Name:_____

Address:_____

City & State:_____Zip:_____

Credit Card #:_____Expires:_____

The Most Recently Published Books

[ ] Send *BJU's Errors on Bible Preservation* by Dr. D. A.
Waite, 120 pages, paperback ($8+$4 S&H) fully indexed

[ ] Send *Romans—Preaching Verse by Verse* by Pastor D. A.
Waite 736 pp. Hardback ($25+$5 S&H) fully indexed

[ ] *Early Manuscripts, Church Fathers, & the Authorized
Version* by Dr. Jack Moorman, $18+$5 S&H. Hardback

[ ] Send *The LIE That Changed the Modern World* by Dr.
H. D. Williams ($16+$5 S&H) Hardback book

[ ] Send *With Tears in My Heart* by Gertrude G. Sanborn.
Hardback 414 pp. ($25+$5 S&H) 400 Christian Poems

Preaching Verse by Verse Books

[ ] Send *Romans—Preaching Verse by Verse* by Pastor D. A.
Waite 736 pp. Hardback ($25+$5 S&H) fully indexed

[ ] Send *Colossians & Philemon—Preaching Verse by Verse* by
Pastor D. A. Waite ($12+$5 S&H) hardback, 240 pages.

[ ] Send *Philippians—Preaching Verse by Verse* by Pastor D.
A. Waite ($10+$5 S&H) hardback, 176 pages.

[ ] Send *Ephesians—Preaching Verse by Verse* by Pastor D. A.
Waite ($12+$5 S&H) hardback, 224 pages.

[ ] Send *Galatians—Preaching Verse By Verse* by Pastor D. A.
Waite ($12+$5 S&H) hardback, 216 pages.

[ ] Send *First Peter—Preaching Verse By Verse* by Pastor D. A.
Waite ($10+$5 S&H) hardback, 176 pages.

Send or Call Orders to:
THE BIBLE FOR TODAY
900 Park Ave., Collingswood, NJ 08108
Phone: 856-854-4452; FAX:--2464; Orders: 1-800 JOHN 10:9
E-Mail Orders: BFT@BibleForToday.org; Credit Cards OK

Order Blank (p. 2)

Name:_____

Address:_____

City & State:_____Zip:_____

Credit Card #:_____Expires:_____

Books on Bible Texts & Translations

[ ] Send *Defending the King James Bible* by Dr. Waite ($12+$5
S&H) A hardback book, indexed with study questions.

[ ] Send *BJU's Errors on Bible Preservation* by Dr. D. A.
Waite, 110 pages, paperback ($8+$4 S&H) fully indexed

[ ] Send *Fundamentalist Deception on Bible Preservation* by
Dr.Waite, ($8+$4 S&H), paperback, fully indexed

[ ] Send *Fundamentalist MIS-INFORMATION on Bible Versions* by Dr. Waite ($7+$4 S&H) perfect bound, 136 pages

[ ] Send *Fundamentalist Distortions on Bible Versions* by Dr.
Waite ($6+$3 S&H) A perfect bound book, 80 pages

[ ] Send *Fuzzy Facts From Fundamentalists* by Dr. D. A.
Waite ($8.00 + $4.00) printed booklet

[ ] Send *Foes of the King James Bible Refuted* by DAW ($10
+$4 S&H) A perfect bound book, 164 pages in length.

[ ] Send *Central Seminary Refuted on Bible Versions* by Dr.
Waite ($10+$4 S&H) A perfect bound book, 184 pages

[ ] Send *The Case for the King James Bible* by DAW ($7
+$3 S&H) A perfect bound book, 112 pages in length.

[ ] Send *Theological Heresies of Westcott and Hort* by Dr. D.
A. Waite, ($7+$3 S&H) A printed booklet.

[ ] Send *Westcott's Denial of Resurrection*, Dr. Waite ($4+$3)

[ ] Send *Four Reasons for Defending KJB* by DAW ($3+$3)

Send or Call Orders to:
THE BIBLE FOR TODAY
900 Park Ave., Collingswood, NJ 08108
Phone: 856-854-4452; FAX:--2464; Orders: 1-800 JOHN 10:9
E-Mail Orders: BFT@BibleForToday.org; Credit Cards OK

Order Blank (p. 3)

Name:_____

Address:_____

City & State:_____Zip:_____

Credit Card #:_____Expires:_____

More Books on Texts & Translations

[ ] Send *Holes in the Holman Christian Standard Bible* by Dr.
Waite ($3+$2 S&H) A printed booklet, 40 pages
[ ] Send *Contemporary Eng. Version Exposed*, DAW ($3+$2)
[ ] Send *NIV Inclusive Language Exposed* by DAW ($5+$3)
[ ] Send *26 Hours of KJB Seminar* (4 videos) by DAW ($50.00)

Books By Dr. Jack Moorman

[ ] *Early Manuscripts, Church Fathers, & the Authorized
Version* by Dr. Jack Moorman, $18+$5 S&H. Hardback
[ ] Send *Forever Settled—Bible Documents & History Survey*
by Dr. Jack Moorman, $20+$5 S&H. Hardback book.
[ ] Send *When the KJB Departs from the So-Called "Majority
Text"* by Dr. Jack Moorman, $16+$5 S&H
[ ] Send *Missing in Modern Bibles—Nestle-Aland & NIV Errors*
by Dr. Jack Moorman, $8+$4 S&H
[ ] Send *The Doctrinal Heart of the Bible—Removed from Mod-
ern Versions* by Dr. Jack Moorman, VCR, $15 +$4 S&H
[ ] Send *Modern Bibles—The Dark Secret* by Dr. Jack Moor-
man, $5+$3 S&H
[ ] Send *Samuel P. Tregelles—The Man Who Made the Critical
Text Acceptable to Bible Believers* by Dr. Moorman ($2+$1)
[ ] Send *8,000 Differences Between TR & CT* by Dr. Jack
Moorman [$65 + $7.50 S&H] Over 500-large-pages of data
[ ] Send *356 Doctrinal Erors in the NIV & Other Modern
Versions*, 100-large-pages, $10.00+$6 S&H.
Send or Call Orders to:
THE BIBLE FOR TODAY
900 Park Ave., Collingswood, NJ 08108
Phone: 856-854-4452; FAX:--2464; Orders: 1-800 JOHN 10:9
E-Mail Orders: BFT@BibleForToday.org; Credit Cards OK

Order Blank (p. 4)

Name:_____

Address:_____

City & State:_____Zip:_____

Credit Card #:_____Expires:_____

Books By or About Dean Burgon

[ ] Send *The Revision Revised* by Dean Burgon ($25 + $5
S&H) A hardback book, 640 pages in length.

[ ] Send *The Last 12 verses of Mark* by Dean Burgon ($15+$5
S&H) A hardback book 400 pages.

[ ] Send *The Traditional Text* hardback by Burgon ($16+$5
S&H) A hardback book, 384 pages in length.

[ ] Send *Causes of Corruption* by Burgon ($15+$5 S&H)
A hardback book, 360 pages in length.

[ ] Send *Inspiration and Interpretation*, Dean Burgon ($25+$5
S&H) A hardback book, 610 pages in length.

[ ] Send *Burgon's Warnings on Revision* by DAW ($7+$4
S&H) A perfect bound book, 120 pages in length.

] Send *Westcott & Hort's Greek Text & Theory Refuted by
Burgon's Revision Revised—Summarized* by Dr. D. A.
Waite ($7.00+$4 S&H), 120 pages, perfect bound.

[ ] Send *Dean Burgon's Confidence in KJB* by DAW ($3+$3)

[ ] Send *Vindicating Mark 16:9-20* by Dr. Waite ($3+$3 S&H)

[ ] Send *Summary of Traditional Text* by Dr. Waite ($3 +$3)

[ ] Send *Summary of Causes of Corruption*, DAW ($3+$3)

[ ] Send *Summary of Inspiration* by Dr. Waite ($3+$3 S&H)

Send or Call Orders to:
THE BIBLE FOR TODAY
900 Park Ave., Collingswood, NJ 08108
Phone: 856-854-4452; FAX:--2464; Orders: 1-800 JOHN 10:9
E-Mail Orders: BFT@BibleForToday.org; Credit Cards OK

Order Blank (p. 5)

Name:_____

Address:_____

City & State:_____Zip:_____

Credit Card #:_____Expires:_____

Books by D. A. Waite, Jr.

[ ] Send *Readability of A.V. (KJB)* by D. A. Waite, Jr. ($6+$3)
[ ] Send *4,114 Definitions from the Defined King James Bible*
    by D. A. Waite, Jr. ($7.00+$4.00 S&H)
[ ] Send *The Doctored New Testament* by D. A. Waite, Jr.
    ($25+$5 S&H) Greek MSS differences shown, hardback
[ ] Send *Defined King James Bible* lg. prt. leather ($40+$7.50)
[ ] Send *Defined King James Bible* med. prt. leather ($35+$6)

Miscellaneous Authors

[ ] Send *Guide to Textual Criticism* by Edward Miller ($7+$4)
    Hardback book
[ ] Send *Scrivener's Greek New Testament Underlying the King
    James Bible*, hardback, ($14+$5 S&H)
[ ] Send *Scrivener's Annotated Greek New Testament*, by Dr.
    Frederick Scrivener: Hardback--($35+$5 S&H);
    Genuine Leather--($45+$5 S&H)
[ ] Send *Why Not the King James Bible?--An Answer to James
    White's KJVO Book* by Dr. K. D. DiVietro, $10+$5 S&H
[ ] Send Brochure #1: "*1000 Titles Defending KJB/TR*"(N.C.)

More Books by Dr. D. A. Waite

[ ] Send *Making Marriage Melodious* by Pastor D. A. Waite
    ($7+$4 S&H), perfect bound, 112 pages.

Send or Call Orders to:
THE BIBLE FOR TODAY
900 Park Ave., Collingswood, NJ 08108
Phone: 856-854-4452; FAX:--2464; Orders: 1-800 JOHN 10:9
E-Mail Orders: BFT@BibleForToday.org; Credit Cards OK

Lightning Source UK Ltd.
Milton Keynes UK
UKOW031833190413

209510UK00009B/73/P